T0301910

An Analysis of

Carole Hillenbrand's

The Crusades:
Islamic Perspectives

Robert Houghton
with
Damien Peters

Published by Macat International Ltd
24:13 Coda Centre, 189 Munster Road, London SW6 6AW.

Distributed exclusively by Routledge
2 Park Square, Milton Park, Abingdon, Oxon OX14 4RN
711 Third Avenue, New York, NY 10017, USA

Routledge is an imprint of the Taylor & Francis Group, an informa business

www.macat.com
info@macat.com

Cataloguing in Publication Data
A catalogue record for this book is available from the British Library.
Library of Congress Cataloguing-in-Publication Data is available upon request.
Cover illustration: Capucine Deslouis

ISBN 978-1-912302-62-8 (hardback)
ISBN 978-1-912128-24-2 (paperback)
ISBN 978-1-912281-50-3 (e-book)

Notice
The information in this book is designed to orientate readers of the work under analysis,
to elucidate and contextualise its key ideas and themes, and to aid in the development
of critical thinking skills. It is not meant to be used, nor should it be used, as a
substitute for original thinking or in place of original writing or research. References and
notes are provided for informational purposes and their presence does not constitute
endorsement of the information or opinions therein. This book is presented solely for
educational purposes. It is sold on the understanding that the publisher is not engaged
to provide any scholarly advice. The publisher has made every effort to ensure that
this book is accurate and up-to-date, but makes no warranties or representations with
regard to the completeness or reliability of the information it contains. The information
and the opinions provided herein are not guaranteed or warranted to produce particular
results and may not be suitable for students of every ability. The publisher shall not be
liable for any loss, damage or disruption arising from any errors or omissions, or from
the use of this book, including, but not limited to, special, incidental, consequential or
other damages caused, or alleged to have been caused, directly or indirectly, by the
information contained within.

CONTENTS

THE MACAT LIBRARY

The Macat Library is a series of unique academic explorations of seminal works in the humanities and social sciences – books and papers that have had a significant and widely recognised impact on their disciplines. It has been created to serve as much more than just a summary of what lies between the covers of a great book. It illuminates and explores the influences on, ideas of, and impact of that book. Our goal is to offer a learning resource that encourages critical thinking and fosters a better, deeper understanding of important ideas.

Each publication is divided into three Sections: Influences, Ideas, and Impact. Each Section has four Modules. These explore every important facet of the work, and the responses to it.

This Section-Module structure makes a Macat Library book easy to use, but it has another important feature. Because each Macat book is written to the same format, it is possible (and encouraged!) to cross-reference multiple Macat books along the same lines of inquiry or research. This allows the reader to open up interesting interdisciplinary pathways.

To further aid your reading, lists of glossary terms and people mentioned are included at the end of this book (these are indicated by an asterisk [*] throughout) – as well as a list of works cited.

Macat has worked with the University of Cambridge to identify the elements of critical thinking and understand the ways in which six different skills combine to enable effective thinking.
Three allow us to fully understand a problem; three more give us the tools to solve it. Together, these six skills make up the **PACIER** model of critical thinking. They are:

ANALYSIS – understanding how an argument is built
EVALUATION – exploring the strengths and weaknesses of an argument
INTERPRETATION – understanding issues of meaning

CREATIVE THINKING – coming up with new ideas and fresh connections
PROBLEM-SOLVING – producing strong solutions
REASONING – creating strong arguments

To find out more, visit **WWW.MACAT.COM.**

CRITICAL THINKING AND
THE CRUSADES: ISLAMIC PERSPECTIVES

Primary critical thinking skill: EVALUATION
Secondary critical thinking skill: ANALYSIS

For many centuries, the history of the crusades, as written by Western historians, was based solidly on Western sources. Evidence from the Islamic societies that the crusaders attacked was used only sparingly – in part because it was hard for most westerners to read, and in part because much of it was inaccessible even for historians who did speak Arabic.

Carole Hillenbrand set out to re-evaluate the sources for the crusading period, not only looking with fresh eyes at known accounts, but also locating and utilizing new sources that had previously been overlooked. Her work involved her in conducting extensive evaluations of the new sources, assessing their arguments, their evidence, and their reasoning in order to assess their value and (using the critical thinking skill of analysis, a powerful method for understanding how arguments are built) to place them correctly in the context of crusade studies as a whole.

The result is not only a history that is more balanced, better argued and more adequate than most that have gone before it, but also a work with relevance for today. At a time when crusading imagery and mentions of the current War on Terror as a 'crusade' help to fuel political narrative, Hillenbrand's evaluative work acts as an important corrective to oversimplification and misrepresentation.

ABOUT THE AUTHOR OF THE ORIGINAL WORK

Carole Hillenbrand is professor of Islamic history at the University of Edinburgh, where she has taught since 1979. Born in England in 1943, she studied as a linguist, becoming fluent in Arabic, Turkish, and Persian, before focusing on medieval Arabic chronicles. Hillenbrand's works cover topics based around the Middle East and medieval Muslim empires. She published *The Crusades: Islamic Perspectives* in 1999, and continues to study and teach the Crusades, Islamic political thought, and the concept of jihad. For her outstanding work, Hillenbrand has been awarded the King Faisal International Prize in Islamic Studies (the first non-Muslim and the first woman to receive it) and has been made an Officer of the Order of the British Empire (OBE).

ABOUT THE AUTHOR OF THE ANALYSIS

Dr Robert Houghton holds a PhD in early medieval history from the University of St Andrews. He is currently a Lecturer in Early Medieval European History at the University of Winchester.

Damien Peters holds an MA in the history of international relations from University College, Dublin.

ABOUT MACAT

GREAT WORKS FOR CRITICAL THINKING

Macat is focused on making the ideas of the world's great thinkers accessible and comprehensible to everybody, everywhere, in ways that promote the development of enhanced critical thinking skills.

It works with leading academics from the world's top universities to produce new analyses that focus on the ideas and the impact of the most influential works ever written across a wide variety of academic disciplines. Each of the works that sit at the heart of its growing library is an enduring example of great thinking. But by setting them in context – and looking at the influences that shaped their authors, as well as the responses they provoked – Macat encourages readers to look at these classics and game-changers with fresh eyes. Readers learn to think, engage and challenge their ideas, rather than simply accepting them.

'Macat offers an amazing first-of-its-kind tool for interdisciplinary learning and research. Its focus on works that transformed their disciplines and its rigorous approach, drawing on the world's leading experts and educational institutions, opens up a world-class education to anyone.'

Andreas Schleicher,
Director for Education and Skills, Organisation for Economic
Co-operation and Development

'Macat is taking on some of the major challenges in university education … They have drawn together a strong team of active academics who are producing teaching materials that are novel in the breadth of their approach.'

Prof Lord Broers,
former Vice-Chancellor of the University of Cambridge

'The Macat vision is exceptionally exciting. It focuses upon new modes of learning which analyse and explain seminal texts which have profoundly influenced world thinking and so social and economic development. It promotes the kind of critical thinking which is essential for any society and economy.
This is the learning of the future.'

Rt Hon Charles Clarke, former UK Secretary of State for Education

'The Macat analyses provide immediate access to the critical conversation surrounding the books that have shaped their respective discipline, which will make them an invaluable resource to all of those, students and teachers, working in the field.'

Professor William Tronzo, University of California at San Diego

WAYS IN TO THE TEXT

KEY POINTS

- The British academic Carole Hillenbrand (b. 1943) has specialized in Eastern languages and medieval Arabic* chronicles for four decades. Arabic was the dominant written language across the Muslim Middle East* during medieval times, and most surviving records are in Arabic.

- Hillenbrand wrote *The Crusades: Islamic Perspectives* (1999) in order to present a range of specifically Muslim historical sources on the Crusades* to a greater audience of non-Arabic speakers. The Crusades were a series of religiously motivated invasions of the region east of the Mediterranean by Christians from Western Europe between 1095 and 1291.

- The Crusades is a unique piece of scholarship as it examines the period of the Crusades solely from Islamic sources. It therefore completely excludes all Western, Byzantine* (Eastern Christian), and Armenian* sources from the same period (the Armenians were a large ethnic group, mostly based in what is now Turkey).

Who Is Carole Hillenbrand?

Carole Hillenbrand, the author of *The Crusades: Islamic Perspectives*, was born in England in 1943 and began her university career in 1962, studying Modern Languages at Girton College, Cambridge. She then moved to Somerville College, Oxford, to study Arabic and Turkish, and later spent a year in Iran from 1969 to 1970 learning the Persian language. A keen linguist, she became fluent in all three languages. During the 1970s, Hillenbrand continued with postgraduate study on Islamic history at the University of Edinburgh in Scotland, focusing on medieval Arabic chronicles. She also produced an edited translation of a medieval Arabic city chronicle, with a commentary.[1]

Hillenbrand became a lecturer in Islamic history at the University of Edinburgh in 1979, and a professor in 2000. She has since been a visiting professor at Dartmouth College, New Hampshire, and the University of Groningen in Holland, and has been an invited lecturer at many Arab universities. Hillenbrand is vice president of the British Society for Middle Eastern Studies, a member of the Council for Assisting Refugee Academics, and edits many Islamic, Persian, and Turkish history books. In 2005, she was awarded the highly prestigious King Faisal International Prize for Islamic Studies,* becoming its first female and first non-Muslim recipient. She was also awarded an OBE* (Order of the British Empire) in 2009,[2] for services to higher education.

Her published works have covered a broad range of historical topics, based around the Middle East (the geographic region roughly containing modern Turkey, Lebanon, Syria, Israel, the Palestinian Territories, Egypt, the Arabian Peninsula, Jordan, Iraq, and Iran). In particular, she has studied the Umayyad Caliphate* and the Artuqid dynasty*: two vast Muslim empires that ruled swathes of Europe and the Middle East in medieval times. Hillenbrand continues to study Turkey and Iran in the medieval period, alongside her work on the Crusades, Islamic political thought, and the concept of jihad.*[3]

"Jihad," which translates as "battle," has been used in many ways in different times and places. Generally, "greater jihad" describes every Muslim's inner spiritual struggle to fulfil his religious duties; "lesser jihad" describes the physical struggle against opponents of Islam (whether this refers to a defensive or an offensive battle against nonbelievers has varied across different eras and cultures). In the context of the Crusades, the term "jihad" was generally used to describe a defensive holy war to reclaim the Holy Land from the invading Crusaders.

Hillenbrand's husband, Robert Hillenbrand,* also works in the University of Edinburgh's department of Islamic and Middle Eastern studies. An honorary professorial fellow, his focus is Islamic art and architecture.

What Does *The Crusades* Say?

The central idea of *The Crusades: Islamic Perspectives* is to introduce readers to new sources on the Crusades.

Briefly, the Crusades were a series of religiously motivated invasions, in which Catholic* Christians from Western Europe invaded the Levant* (in medieval times a vast region in the Eastern Mediterranean and Middle East). The Crusades began in 1095, after the Byzantine Empire,* a Christian kingdom in the Middle East, was invaded by (Muslim) Seljuk Turks.* The Byzantine emperor appealed to the Catholic pope, Urban II,* for assistance. Urban saw an opportunity to reunite the Catholic Church and the Eastern Christians, and to reclaim the holy city of Jerusalem, which had been seized from Christian control by Arabic forces in the seventh century. He urged Western Catholics to wage an "armed pilgrimage," offering absolution from sin as a reward. Tens of thousands of armed Catholics reclaimed or seized large areas of southern Anatolia, Syria, and Palestine from the Muslims, including Jerusalem, and established "Crusader states"* to govern them. For two centuries, Western Catholics constantly took the Crusader vow and traveled to defend the Holy Land, with larger, more organized campaigns occurring about once a generation, usually in order to counter a Muslim advance or other crisis. In spite of this, the Crusader states were gradually reclaimed by Islamic forces and, apart from a few scattered islands, the last remnants were defeated in 1291.

At the time of publication of *The Crusades* in 1999, most other histories of the Crusades only used Western sources. Hillenbrand's wide-ranging research unearthed many previously undiscovered or untranslated texts and references to the Crusades in the Islamic world, which were collected and included in the work.

While not the first book to do this, *The Crusades* used more of these authorities than any other text. The subtitle—*Islamic Perspectives*—refers neatly to Hillenbrand's primary goal in writing. Specifically, she sought to present Muslim sources for the Crusades to an audience that had not been exposed to these documents in any great depth, both non-Muslims and Muslims who were not able to read Arabic.[4] Further, by locating and utilizing sources that had not been used before, Hillenbrand provided access to new materials for Arabic Muslims.[5]

It is worth noting that, in the Arab world, there were no medieval histories written in Arabic that focused solely on the Crusades, and in most Arab histories the Crusades are only mentioned briefly as they were largely overshadowed in the region by other large wars and invasions. Modern Arabic histories that deal with the Crusades use a much narrower base of sources and are criticized by Hillenbrand as being deliberately, and sometimes aggressively, critical of the West. At the time of writing, *The Crusades* is still the best reference for Islamic sources on the Crusades.

Two years after the book's publication, the attacks of September 11, 2001 (9/11*) took place, in which the Islamic terrorist group al-Qaeda* killed 2,996 people after hijacking passenger jets, triggering America's later invasions of Afghanistan and Iraq. This made Hillenbrand's text particularly topical, as it explained how widespread misunderstandings of the Crusades persist even now, in both the Western and Islamic worlds. In the past, certain governments have used the Crusades as propaganda;* the Iraqi dictator Saddam Hussein* and Libyan dictator Muammar Gaddafi,* for example, both referred to Western governments and armies as "Crusaders." These misrepresentations only increased with the waging of the War on Terror,* the name given by the American government to the US-led military campaigns around the world after the 9/11 attacks.

Hillenbrand intended her work to correct these false accounts. *It explains* how many of the accepted set of narratives and historical beliefs regarding the Crusades were in fact entirely inaccurate and demonstrates the increasing importance that universities now place on Islamic sources. *The Crusades* is on the reading lists for modules at Cambridge and St Andrews universities and Hillenbrand's academic influence has been illustrated by the publication of a volume of academic essays dedicated to her, *Living Islamic History* (2010).

The Crusades is divided into five themes (or sections), all designed to illustrate her central argument that Islamic sources can provide extensive evidence about the Middle East during the Crusades. The first focuses on the impact of the First Crusade, and the arrival of the Western Europeans, in the Middle East. In the second section, Hillenbrand addresses the ways that jihad was presented as a physical struggle against the opponents of Islam (as opposed to an inner spiritual struggle) from the establishment of the Crusader states and the subsequent Muslim counterattacks (between 1100 and 1174) up to the final Muslim reconquest of the last Crusader cities in 1291.

Hillenbrand's third section studies Islamic portrayals of life in the Holy Land, Muslim perceptions of the Crusaders and relations between the Crusaders and Muslims. In the fourth, she reveals Islamic accounts of warfare and other military concerns in the Levant. Finally, in the fifth, she considers how modern Islamic authors and political and cultural organizations have employed the idea of the Crusades. She also suggests that an understanding of the modern Islamic world, and its attitudes toward the West, can be gained by considering the Crusades from both the medieval and modern Islamic perspectives.

Why Does *The Crusades* Matter?

Even Hillenbrand's critics generally view *The Crusades* as a valuable addition to the existing scholarship. Her text remains important for the breadth of new material it considers, particularly in a field dominated for decades by one-sided accounts, and "definitive" texts that told only half a story. While more recent books offer simpler introductions to the period, Hillenbrand's work remains, even now, the primary reference for many Islamic sources that would otherwise be unavailable. As a result, she has influenced many other writers of the Crusades and their readers, in addition to the generations of university students who have studied her text.

The usefulness of *The Crusades* is enhanced by current and ongoing trends around the subject. Individual sections of the text are of great importance to historians of different topics. For example, Hillenbrand's considerations of the motives and depictions of jihad in the Middle Ages*—the period dating roughly from the fall of the Roman Empire in the West (circa 500 C.E.) to the period of European cultural history known as the Renaissance* (circa 1400)— will be of interest to military and political historians. Meanwhile, her chapters on day-to-day life in the medieval Levant will be of most concern to social and gender historians. Also of interest is her research on the interaction between the Muslims and Franks* (in Crusades studies, the term "Franks" refers to all Crusaders, regardless of their nationality.)

For the general reader, the most important theme is likely to be how the Crusades are presented in public discourse (films, literature, and debate, for example) and writings in the contemporary Muslim world. In Hillenbrand's text, this element provides a powerful connection between the current political situation in the Middle East and the wider world, and the study of Islamic sources on the Crusades.

Hillenbrand's book has also made an impact in many fields beyond medieval and Islamic history. *The Crusades* has been cited by academics in fields as diverse as terrorism, racism, teaching, and medicine. The utility of the text—to readers from any field—lies in the fact that her basic ideas are relatively simple and in line with current modes of scholarly thought on the Crusades. Her ideas could also help to create more collaboration between Western and Muslim scholars. Should this happen, *The Crusades* could become a tool for altering and strengthening the links between academic communities.

NOTES

1   Queen Mary University of London, "Resources for Studying the Crusades," accessed May 30, 2013, http://www.crusaderstudies.org.uk/resources/historians/profiles/hillenbrand/.

2   University of Edinburgh, "Professor Carole Hillenbrand," accessed December 10, 2015, http://www.ed.ac.uk/literatures-languages-cultures/islamic-middle-eastern/people/c-hillenbrand.

3   University of Edinburgh, "Professor Carole Hillenbrand."

4   Carole Hillenbrand, *The Crusades: Islamic Perspectives* (Edinburgh: Edinburgh University Press, 1999), 3.

5   Hillenbrand, *The Crusades*, 9–10.

SECTION 1
INFLUENCES

MODULE 1
THE AUTHOR AND THE
HISTORICAL CONTEXT

KEY POINTS

- While more recent works provide broader and more accessible introductions to the series of religiously motivated invasions of the Middle East* by Christian armies from Western Europe between 1095 and 1291, known as the Crusades,* Hillenbrand's text remains relevant as a key point of reference, particularly as it contains so many previously underused or undiscovered Islamic texts.

- Hillenbrand is a skilled linguist, fluent in Arabic,* Persian, and Turkish, among other languages. This gives her access to a wealth of non-Western historical sources that are closed off to most of her peers.

- Hillenbrand wrote *The Crusades* (1999) during a time of increasing political and social interest in the Middle East, and after a series of clashes between Western and Muslim interests. These clashes would culminate in the terrorist attacks of 9/11* two years after the book was published, and the subsequent War on Terror* launched by the United States in response.

Why Read this Text?

In the years since the publication of Carole Hillenbrand's *The Crusades: Islamic Perspectives*, no historical work has emerged to match its depth and range of Islamic sources. Many of these sources had been largely unknown in the wider academic world, even to other modern scholars considering the subject from an Islamic outlook. For academics and

❝ During these days of heightened tension in the Middle East, for many the Crusades have taken on an urgency, as a distant historical phenomenon that speaks powerfully to present religious and political concerns. ❞

Dawn Marie Hayes, *Harnessing the Potential in Historiography and Popular Culture When Teaching the Crusades*

students seeking an incisive insight into the Islamic world during the Crusades, Hillenbrand's text remains a vital work. This is particularly the case for those who are seeking a postcolonialist* viewpoint.

Postcolonialist scholars argue that most Western academics are guilty of "colonial" bias: that is, they perpetuate imperialist* ideas and imagery in their discussion of Eastern cultures, even well after the end of the colonial era ("imperialism" here refers to the policy of building an empire, commonly by means of establishing colonies in foreign territories). As a result, the work of these Western academics cannot present a fully realistic and accurate portrayal of Middle Eastern history. Postcolonialists aim to broaden understanding by placing greater emphasis on the accounts produced by non-Western authors.

The dominant position of Islamic scholarship, meanwhile, both in the West and Islamic countries, has been to view the Crusades in the same light as twentieth-century colonial periods in the Middle East. As a consequence, the Crusades are analyzed in conjunction with events that took place centuries later. By contrast, in *The Crusades*, Hillenbrand allows the voices of Middle Eastern inhabitants who actually lived during the Crusades to be heard without the distortion of subsequent events. The book therefore challenges traditional schools of historical thought both in the West and the Muslim world. It also provides a counter to Western orientalism* (a term generally used to describe a patronizing perspective that only considers Western viewpoints, as shown by Western scholars when studying the rest of the world, particularly the East).

As a reference work, *The Crusades* remains unmatched, and it is widely cited in medieval and Crusade-related historiography* (the aims, methods, and practice of writing history), as well as in fields as diverse as racism studies[1] and medicine.[2]

Author's Life

Born in England in 1943, Carole Hillenbrand began her university career studying modern languages at Girton College, Cambridge, focusing on European languages, learning French, German, Old French, and Medieval Latin. After graduating, she moved to Somerville College, Oxford, and from 1968 to 1972 she studied Eastern languages, including Persian (the language of Iran today), for which she spent a year in Iran. Among other languages, Hillenbrand is now fully fluent in Arabic, Persian, and Turkish; Arabic was the primary language of Islamic scholarship for more than a thousand years. In 1972 she moved to the University of Edinburgh to study medieval Islamic history at postgraduate level. During her studies she produced an edited translation, with a commentary, of a medieval Arabic city chronicle, under the supervision of the historian John Walsh.[3]

Hillenbrand began lecturing in Islamic history at Edinburgh in 1979, and became professor of Islamic history in 2000, the position she holds today. Hillenbrand has also been a visiting professor at Dartmouth College in the US state of New Hampshire, and at the University of Groningen, Netherlands. Her outstanding work has been recognized in both the Muslim and Western worlds: in 2005, she was the first female and non-Muslim to receive the King Faisal International Prize in Islamic Studies* in Saudi Arabia and in 2009 she was made an officer of the Order of the British Empire (OBE*).[4]

Robert Hillenbrand,* her husband, also works at Edinburgh University's department of Islamic and Middle Eastern studies, focusing on Islamic art and architecture. His influence can be seen in

The Crusades,[5] which includes a large selection of illustrations. Hillenbrand explains that she sees these illustrations as a "subtext" with a story of their own that stands outside the literary descriptions of her written sources. She writes that they "set the text in a visual context that would invoke the medieval Levant"* and also "fill the multiple gaps left by the medieval Islamic sources."[6]

Author's Background

At the University of Edinburgh, Hillenbrand has been influenced by her husband and other colleagues, such as the professor of Arabic Yasir Suleiman.* It was the former's influence that saw her include Islamic art and illustrations in her work to broaden the narrative of her text, and the latter whose work on Arabic sources encouraged Hillenbrand to go further with *The Crusades* than had been done before. In her introduction, she characterizes Suleiman's assistance as "invaluable."

In the wider context, Hillenbrand wrote *The Crusades* at a time of increasing political and social interest in the Middle East. Muslim scholars were becoming increasingly active and visible in the West throughout the 1990s. There were also a series of clashes between Western and Muslim interests, such as the 1998 bombings of the US embassies in Kenya and Tanzania by the fundamental Islamic terrorist group al-Qaeda.* There is no doubt that her ideas were affected by these political trends and the scholarly debates that accompanied them.

The Crusades is original in one specific aspect of its approach to the Crusades—Hillenbrand makes it clear at the book's outset that "only Islamic perspectives will be discussed" within it.[7] Hillenbrand's text was the first extensive study of the Crusades to take this approach, and it marks a conscious move away from traditional Western historiography, which has usually viewed the Crusades from the perspective of the Crusaders and their own chroniclers. The Crusades were largely forgotten in the Islamic world for many centuries after they ended, as they were regarded as being of little importance compared to greater invasions, such as those of the Mongols* (a nomadic central Asian people who established a Eurasian empire in the thirteenth century). As a result, few historical accounts were written—and in more recent times, even Arab scholars have treated the Crusades as precursors for the much later eras of Western colonialism. By considering the perspective of the contemporary Muslim victims of the Crusades, Hillenbrand creates a consideration of the events and attitudes of the period that is broader and more balanced than was previously possible.

It should be noted, however, that some historians, such as the Italian Francesco Gabrieli* and the Lebanese French Amin Maalouf,* had made attempts to incorporate accounts of the Crusades from the Muslim perspective into their work. Their books *Arab Historians of the Crusades* (1957) and *The Crusades Through Arab Eyes* (1983), respectively, represent early attempts to highlight Islamic sources by Western scholars.

NOTES

1   M. Shahid Alam et al., "Eurocentrism, Sinocentrism and World History: A Symposium," *Science & Society* 67, no. 2 (Summer 2003): 173–217.

2   Harry Brewer, "Historical Perspectives on Health: Early Arabic Medicine," *The Journal of the Royal Society for the Promotion of Health* 124.4 (2004): 184–7.

3   Queen Mary University of London, "Resources for Studying the Crusades," accessed May 30, 2013, http://www.crusaderstudies.org.uk/resources/historians/profiles/hillenbrand/.

4   University of Edinburgh, "Professor Carole Hillenbrand," accessed May 30, 2013, http://www.ed.ac.uk/literatures-languages-cultures/islamic-middle-eastern/people/c-hillenbrand.

5   University of Edinburgh, "Professor Robert Hillenbrand," accessed May 31, 2013, http://www.ed.ac.uk/literatures-languages-cultures/islamic-middle-eastern/people/r-hillenbrand.

6   Carole Hillenbrand, *The Crusades: Islamic Perspectives* (Edinburgh: Edinburgh University Press, 1999), xi.

7   Hillenbrand, *The Crusades*, 2.

MODULE 2
ACADEMIC CONTEXT

KEY POINTS

- Postcolonial* historians of the Crusade* period (that is, academics who reject understandings of the world with their roots in the colonial period), have sought to broaden understanding of the era by placing greater emphasis on accounts produced by non-Western authors.

- Modern histories of the Crusades include a much greater presentation of sources from authors originating from non-European backgrounds.

- Hillenbrand's *The Crusades* was the first dedicated history of the Crusades to be produced entirely from Islamic sources.

The Work In Its Context

Carole Hillenbrand's *The Crusades: Islamic Perspectives* has emerged from a broader postcolonial movement in Crusades studies that seeks to place greater emphasis on the accounts produced by non-Western authors. Since the 1970s, the postcolonial movement has challenged the traditional and popular Western views of the Crusades. The result is a drive within Western scholarship to move away from the Eurocentric* views of the nineteenth and early twentieth century. (Eurocentrism is a perspective on the world's history and culture that is based mainly—or entirely—on Western viewpoints; it was the norm in Western academia until the mid-twentieth century, and many academics and politicians are still accused of it today.)

Hillenbrand criticized the state of Islamic history writing on the Crusades; she cited both the dearth of coverage on this era in Arab histories, and the severe underuse of Arab sources even by Arab writers,

❝ This book is the first full-length monographic [that is, an academic study on one small area of learning] treatment of the Crusades as seen by the Muslims. **❞**

Carole Hillenbrand, *The Crusades: Islamic Perspectives*

whom she says are mired in nineteenth-century thinking and fond of endlessly reusing the same sources. With the importance of the Middle East* growing through the 1990s, Hillenbrand felt that the time was right for a dedicated work that accurately explored contemporary Islamic perceptions of the Crusades, and she aimed her text at academics and nonacademics alike.

The Crusades is intended to counter misrepresentations of the Crusades, starting with the misappropriation of the word itself in current popular culture; "Crusaders" is used as a term of anti-Western abuse in modern Islamic propaganda, while, in the West, "Crusade" is used to describe a noble struggle.

Hillenbrand relates these misrepresentations to contemporary issues, such as the use of jihadi* propaganda* in Muslim states. "Jihadi propaganda" is designed to provoke people to violent acts; it commonly uses the victories of the medieval Islamic armies that reclaimed the Crusader states* as a rallying cry for modern believers to engage in "jihad" (battle) against the West.

She also refers to orientalist* tendencies (that is, patronising and Eurocentric attitudes to the rest of the world) within Western scholarship and politics[1] which, she says, is illustrated by noting the miniscule number of Crusade historians who have bothered to learn Arabic. To rectify this, she argues that modern accounts of the Crusades need to place sufficient emphasis on the evidence provided by Muslim authors of the Crusading period, to give the reader as thorough and unbiased a study as possible.

Hillenbrand intended the work to be of use to those specializing in the Crusading period (circa 1099–1291) in the Middle East, and she aimed to reach Muslim scholars, particularly those who could not read Arabic, as well as non-Muslim historians.[2] *The Crusades* is designed to challenge the expectations of its audience—who had been used to Crusade histories being little more than overviews and timelines of battles and ideological conflicts—by providing access to materials that had not previously been available. By highlighting Arabic sources, including several that had formerly existed only in manuscript form, Hillenbrand presents her audience with a new range of underexploited materials with which to study the Crusades.

Overview of the Field

In recent times, twentieth-century Western scholars of the Crusades, such as the British historians Steven Runciman* and Geoffrey Barraclough,* have abandoned the older, positive views of the Crusades. While they now condemn the events that they describe, their work nevertheless only focuses on the experiences of the Crusaders, ignoring those of the peoples they invaded. Hillenbrand deliberately challenged this tendency, along with a similar practice in the Islamic world to downplay the importance of the Turks during the period, a consequence of residual resentment for the subject status of Arab peoples under the Turkish Ottoman Empire.

Hillenbrand's work was inspired in part by several of her colleagues, including Jonathan Riley-Smith,* a prominent British Crusades historian. In her introduction to *The Crusades,* Hillenbrand cites Riley-Smith's criticism of those who study the Crusades without considering the Islamic sources, and those who study the Muslim world without considering the Crusades.[3] Her techniques of close textual analysis have been influenced by Israeli historian Emmanuel Sivan,* author of "Modern Arab Historiography of the Crusades" (1972), and Donald Richards,* a longtime British advocate of the use of Islamic sources in the writing of history, who was Hillenbrand's professor while she was a student at Oxford.[4]

More generally, her work embraces the long-standing postcolonialist* arguments promoted by authors such as Edward Said.* A Palestinian American literary critic, Said was outspoken in his criticism of Western historians for perpetuating imperialist* ideas and imagery in their discussion of Eastern cultures. These imperialist ideas persisted in academic studies long after the end of the colonial era, resulting in work that struggled to present a realistic and accurate portrayal of Middle Eastern history.

While Hillenbrand acknowledges this, she also highlights the prevalence of a "reverse orientalism" among many Islamic scholars. Hillenbrand argues that they are guilty of comparing Western involvement in the medieval Middle East (that is, the Crusades) both with late nineteenth-century Western imperialism in the same region, and recent events such as the 2003 US-led invasion of Iraq (Iraq War*). Ironically, these Islamic scholars have developed their theories using the very ideas and narratives that "orientalist" Western scholars had formulated to frame their own postcolonial narratives.

In short, in both "orientalist" and "counterorientalist" schools of thought, there is a direct link between the violent foundation of the original Crusader states,* the establishment of European colonies during the nineteenth and early twentieth century, the creation of the state of Israel on previously Arab territory in 1948, and finally, the modern wars of the early twenty-first century in Afghanistan and Iraq.

For example, Hillenbrand states that in the hands of historians such as Muhammad al-'Arusi al-Matwi,* the Crusades were transformed into a sort of "protocolonialism" and the Crusader states "protocolonies" (essentially framing the Crusades as the first stages in a longer-term campaign of colonization). However, this flies in the face of the authentic contemporary Muslim thinking on the nature of the Crusaders' presence in the Levant* at the time.[5] Hillenbrand argues that the Crusades must be studied without the muddying and anachronistic effect that modern comparisons bring (an anachronism is something mistakenly placed in a time where it does not belong.) She states that the notions of modern international relations and even religiosity bear no relation to those of centuries before, when such concepts did not exist.

Academic Influences

Perhaps the most immediate of Hillenbrand's academic influences is her husband and fellow academic Robert Hillenbrand,* who has worked extensively on medieval Islamic art and architecture,[6] and whose input encouraged her to incorporate numerous art and architectural sources into her text.[7]

There is an informal school of scholars in Crusades studies, whose members include Jonathan Riley-Smith, that seeks to incorporate non-Western perspectives into the study of the field. The school has been influenced by the broader postcolonialist movement that advocates greater consideration of non-Western perspectives across all scholarships. This modernizing group of Crusades scholars has had a large impact on the structure and content of Hillenbrand's text. In return, her work has provided more impetus and input to their movement.

The influences that shine through most noticeably in Hillenbrand's text, however, are those of the medieval Islamic chroniclers and historians quoted throughout. In her translations and accompanying commentaries, she includes the voices of men who recorded the events of the Islamic world when it was at its peak of technological and philosophical output, such as Ali ibn al-Athir* (1160–1223), an Arabic historian who followed Saladin* (circa 1137–93), the powerful Islamic leader who defeated the Crusader states and reclaimed Jerusalem. Ali ibn al-Athir wrote a key world history book, *The Universal History*, which was largely inaccessible until translated by Hillenbrand.

In *The Crusades*, she successfully paints a portrait of how the people living in the shadow of the Crusades actually got on with their lives, making the best of situations patently beyond their control and compromising, as people do, without the baggage of ideology or aggression that modern accounts imagine them to have carried.

NOTES

1   Carole Hillenbrand, *The Crusades: Islamic Perspectives* (Edinburgh: Edinburgh University Press, 1999), 248.

2   Hillenbrand, *The Crusades*, 3.

3   Hillenbrand, *The Crusades*, 3.

4   Hillenbrand, *The Crusades*, xxxix, 12–13.

5   Hillenbrand, *The Crusades*, 614.

6   University of Edinburgh, "Professor Robert Hillenbrand," accessed May 31, 2013, http://www.ed.ac.uk/literatures-languages-cultures/islamic-middle-eastern/people/r-hillenbrand.

7   Hillenbrand, *The Crusades*, xl.

MODULE 3
THE PROBLEM

KEY POINTS

- The core question of *The Crusades* is: What can the Islamic sources of the period tell us about the Crusades* and the Muslim experience of the Crusades?

- Western scholars have traditionally presented the Crusades only from the perspective of the Crusaders, causing limitations and bias.

- Hillenbrand uses a systematic and thematic technique to address a number of topics in relation to the Islamic sources, and to discuss how they can be used to further our understanding of the Crusades.

Core Question

The core question that Carole Hillenbrand sets out to answer in *The Crusades: Islamic Perspectives* is: What can the Islamic sources of the period tell us about the Crusades, and about the Muslim experience of the Crusades? This is important because historiography* relating to the Crusades produced in the West, and even the Muslim world, has often failed to address the Islamic sources. While Islamic histories have frequently skimmed over the Crusades, Western works have relied solely on Western sources, with contemporary materials produced by Muslims and other groups in the Middle East* being used only rarely and in an auxiliary role. This has led to the production of a distorted and incomplete picture of events in the period.

The objective of *The Crusades* is not intellectually controversial. In fact, there is general agreement in modern Crusades studies that Islamic sources need to be considered in greater depth. However, it is telling that although Hillenbrand and her colleagues had spent decades

❝ On the Western side, those who write about the Crusades and who do not read Arabic (which is the vast majority of scholars) depend for their knowledge of the Muslim sources on translations which cover the field in a patchy and unsatisfactory way. ❞

Carole Hillenbrand, *The Crusades: Islamic Perspectives*

working in the historiographical area of translating and analyzing Medieval Islamic texts, no other work of similar size and scope to *The Crusades* had appeared during those years.

Meanwhile, the histories of the Crusades that had been published often employed a long, narrative style, without sufficient analysis or commentary. Often, the authors had neglected to include what could be classified as important works by medieval Islamic authors, due to their inaccessibility. The difficulty in actually obtaining and using these sources is highlighted by the fact that Hillenbrand herself was only afforded access to a copy of the *Kitab al-Jihad** (*Book of War/Struggle*) by the Syrian scholar Ali ibn Tahir al-Sulami* at the last moment, thereby enabling it to be included in her text. This treatise, published in 1105, was the first to preach jihad* (in this context, a defensive battle) against the newly arrived Christian Crusaders, calling for a coordinated Muslim counterattack. Several other texts included in the book, such as the twelfth- and thirteenth-century historian Ali ibn al-Athir's* *Universal History,* had previously been largely unavailable to Western and Muslim scholars due to the lack of an acceptable translation. Yet both of these works were essential for building a complete narrative of the evolution of Arabic thought on the Crusades, and concepts such as jihad, from the fall of Jerusalem in 1099 to the end of the Crusader presence on the mainland Levant* in 1291.

Without these contemporary Islamic accounts and the unique

insights they provide, the understanding of one of the most formative periods in both Western and Islamic history (two civilizations making up roughly half the world's population) would have stayed rooted in one of two understandings: either the outmoded thinking of nineteenth- and twentieth-century colonialist* historians in the West, or the emotional anticolonial* rhetoric that developed in the East.

The Participants

There are three schools of thought on the Crusades that Hillenbrand wished to challenge. The first comprised the Western authors who still focus narrowly on the experience of the Crusaders themselves.[1] Second were the postcolonial* thinkers such as Edward Said,* who argued both that Islamic voices should be heard, and that the Crusades were simply one part of a long-established Western orientalist* perspective.

Said's term "orientalism" denotes a Western understanding of the "Orient" as a "semi-mythical construct" or "other," which is then "made and re-made countless times" to fit the latest narrative of whichever non-Orientals are writing the history.[2] Said argues that this thinking dates as far back as the Greco–Persian Wars* of the fifth and fourth centuries B.C.E. and continued until the twentieth century and the mandate* system (in which countries, ostensibly freed from occupation and control after World War I,* were placed under the governorship of Western countries; although officially independent, mandate countries essentially became imperial* possessions.)

The third school of thought criticized by Hillenbrand comprised Middle Eastern scholars such as Fayid Hammad Muhammad 'Ashur* and Suhayl Zakkar,* whom she claimed ignored the Islamic sources. Instead, she argues, they primarily presented the Crusades as early manifestations of modern Western colonialism and imperialism.[3]

While coverage of the Crusades in the more mainstream media was yet to reach the levels that occurred following the 9/11* terrorist attacks on America, the debate was nevertheless quite prominent in the 1990s, leading to Hillenbrand's decision to write her text. Middle Eastern rulers who were both Islamic and opposed the policies of the West, such as the Iraqi dictator Saddam Hussein* and the Libyan dictator Muammar Gaddafi,* often evoked negative imagery of the Crusades in propaganda* and referred disparagingly to Western governments, soldiers, and leaders as "Crusaders."[4] Conversely, in the West, the term "Crusade" was used to describe a noble and positive undertaking or struggle, applicable even in fields such as sport or politics. Both of these limited viewpoints are challenged by the accounts that Hillenbrand has gathered in *The Crusades*. The book clearly contradicts the idea that Crusaders were either unfailingly noble or unfailingly immoral. It also proves that, in fact, Christians and Muslims often coexisted peacefully in the Crusader states.

The Contemporary Debate

While the narrative and central arguments of *The Crusades* remained topical and important in the year following its 1999 publication, the book began to take on a more pronounced immediacy with the outbreak of the Second Intifada* in Israel and Palestine in September 2000. This was an uprising by Palestinians against Israeli policy that resulted in a wave of violence and thousands of deaths. In *The Crusades*, Hillenbrand addresses the way certain Arabs and Islamists view the state of Israel as the inheritor of the legacy of the Crusades, despite the difference in the respective religions of the settlers. She also relates how modern Arab accounts tend to echo those of the Arabs who lived during violent periods of the Crusades.[5] For example, the Palestinian poet and novelist Mahmud Darwish* referred to Israeli troops as "leftover Crusaders" in his writings.

The topicality of the Crusades, and the question of how modern audiences should interpret them, reached unprecedented levels after the terrorist attacks committed by Islamic extremists on 9/11. This was highlighted days after the attacks when the American president,

George W. Bush,* used the term "Crusade," as he announced the launch of the so-called War on Terror.* This involved US-led invasions of Afghanistan* and Iraq,* and Bush's use of the word evoked embarrassment in Europe and anger in the Islamic world.[6]

In the early 2000s the events of the Crusades, and particularly what they meant to modern-day Muslims, became questions that went beyond academic interpretations. Instead they transformed, quite literally, into questions of life and death. Hillenbrand's book was one of the few places where an answer could be found.

NOTES

1   Steven Runciman, *A History of the Crusades*, vol. 3 (Cambridge: Cambridge University Press, 1951–54), 480; Geoffrey Barraclough, "Deus le Volt?" *New York Review of Books*, May 21, 1970, accessed December 10, 2015, http://www.nybooks.com/articles/1970/05/21/deus-le-volt/.

2   Edward Said, *Orientalism* (London: Vintage, 1978), xviii, 58.

3   Suhayl Zakkar, *Madkhal ila ta'riikh al-hurub al-salibiyah* (Introduction to the history of the Crusades) (Beirut: Dar al-Fikr, 1973); F. H. M. 'Ashur, *Al-jihad al-islami didd al-salibiyyan wa'l-murghul fi'l-'asr al-mamluk* (Islamic jihad against the Crusaders and Mongols in the Mamluk period) (Tripoli, Lebanon: Jros Press, 1995).

4   Carole Hillenbrand, *The Crusades: Islamic Perspectives* (Edinburgh: Edinburgh University Press, 1999), 610.

5   Hillenbrand, *The Crusades,* 613.

6   Peter Ford, "Europe cringes at Bush 'crusade' against terrorists," *Christian Science Monitor*, September 19, 2001, accessed December 10, 2015, http://www.csmonitor.com/2001/0919/p12s2-woeu.html.

MODULE 4
THE AUTHOR'S CONTRIBUTION

KEY POINTS

- In *The Crusades* Hillenbrand collected and translated contemporary Arabic* sources on the Crusades,* many of which had previously been inaccessible to non-Arabic speakers.

- Hillenbrand's text allowed a great deal of information to be examined for the first time by a much broader audience.

- The need to incorporate non-European perspectives into the writing of history, particularly into those dealing with the Middle East,* had been highlighted as early as the 1970s.

Author's Aims

Carole Hillenbrand's *The Crusades: Islamic Perspectives* is an attempt to introduce a range of hitherto unknown or underused Islamic sources to a new audience, both in the West and the Islamic world itself. Using these sources, she is able to reinterpret the Crusades in a way that moves beyond the limitations of an approach in which historical analysis is conducted by comparing modern events to examples from the colonial* history of worldwide empire-building. Hillenbrand aims to avoid these limitations and see each historical event in isolation, within its own circumstances.

Hillenbrand reveals that the interfaith relations of the Crusading period were not invariably antagonistic, as is usually assumed. In fact, for Muslims, the book offers a revelatory new narrative, using twelfth- and thirteenth-century Islamic scholars and writers to show that the Crusades were not an era of unremitting warfare or strife, that in fact there were periods of peaceful coexistence between Christians and

> ❝ The landmark work of Carole Hillenbrand, along with an increasing number of texts in translation, is beginning to allow a fuller and clearer appreciation of the impact of the Crusades in the Eastern Mediterranean. ❞
>
> Jonathan Phillips, *The Crusades 1095–1197*

Muslims. Hillenbrand also uses her sources to explore daily life in the Crusader states* for both Muslims and Christians, the lives of women, and the evolution of understandings of the term "jihad."*

In her introduction Hillenbrand states that the book is primarily intended for students and the general public, with a hope that specialists will also find it interesting. However, she also makes it clear that *The Crusades* is meant to serve as a "salutary" (beneficial) lesson for those non-Muslims who live in a modern, secular age. She hopes that they will gain an understanding of how so much of the modern world that we see around us has been formed by the clash between two medieval religious ideologies. Indeed, it was no doubt eye-opening for many readers to learn quite how large a role religion and faith played in the lives and decisions of medieval peoples. Even more surprising, in this age when Islamist* violence (violence provoked by the ideology associated with politically radicalized Islamic teaching) and declarations of jihad (frequently associated in popular culture today with reference to a war of attack against unbelievers and heretics) make headlines on a daily basis, would be the lesson at the heart of *The Crusades*—that it was the Christians, not Muslims, who were the violent fanatics of the medieval period.

Approach

The departure from conventional Crusader narratives is made early in the text, when Hillenbrand examines the initial Muslim responses to the First Crusade.* This took place between 1096 and 1099, after

Pope Urban II's* rallying call for Western Catholics* to join an "armed pilgrimage" to assist besieged Eastern Christians in the Byzantine Empire* (a large political body in this period centered around present-day Turkey with territories all around the eastern Mediterranean). The Crusade was extremely successful, and led to the establishment of Catholic kingdoms in the lands the Crusaders occupied, described nowadays as the Crusader states.* While this was most often presented as being a disaster for the people of the Levant,*[1] culminating in a massacre of non-Christians after the capture of Jerusalem in 1099, Hillenbrand's sources are unequivocal in stating that for most Arabs "the response to the coming of the Crusades was … one of apathy, compromise, and preoccupation with internal problems."[2]

Hillenbrand uses her sources to paint a picture of a highly developed and civilized Islamic people throughout the wider region, who were bewildered by the arrival of a group of people with whom they had no previous interaction. For example, instead of a vigorous counterattack after the fall of Jerusalem, the response was slow to develop because the Muslim world was consumed with internal squabbles. Consequently, it took decades for Muslim leaders to develop a response to the Frankish* armies (the Crusaders) and their states. But, eventually, they combined to form an anti-Crusader ideology that resurrected the outmoded notion of jihad as meaning a definitive fight against opponents of the Muslim faith, instead of an inner spiritual struggle.

Next, Hillenbrand discusses the experiences of both Crusaders and Muslims during two centuries of Crusader occupation and settlement in the region. These sections depart from the Western, orientalist,* and colonialist narratives that traditionally dominated the field, such as the belief that the Muslims were uniformly opposed to the Crusaders. Hillenbrand corrects this half-truth by analyzing the nonpolitical written and artistic accounts of the time. For example, she relates how the twelfth-century pilgrim Ibn Jubayr* realized that

Muslims living under Frankish rule were actually better off than their nonsubjugated neighbors, and were therefore happy to continue with the arrangement of Frankish governance of their land.[3] This conclusion is perhaps one of the most unconventional aspects of *The Crusades*.

Contribution in Context

To understand how influential Hillenbrand's book has been, it is important to consider the history of the Middle East during the twentieth century—the period during which most histories of the Crusades were written. Following widespread conflict in the region during World War I,* much of the Middle East was occupied by Britain and France. During the war, the British government had given the Arab leaders guarantees that a unified Arab state would be formed, but this never actually materialized. Instead, Britain and France divided up the Turkish and Ottoman provinces to create a set of entirely new countries. Britain took control of Palestine, Jordan, and Iraq, while France took over Syria and Lebanon. These new countries were rubber-stamped with the veneer of legitimacy by the League of Nations* (an international body replaced by the United Nations in 1945) and held as mandates:* territories controlled until such time as they were judged competent to rule themselves. Unknown to the Arab leaders, Britain had also guaranteed the leaders of the Zionist* movement (a movement most active in the late nineteenth and early twentieth century that lobbied for the establishment of a Jewish homeland in Palestine) that it would later assist them in their goal to establish a Jewish state within the borders of Palestine.

The Arabs, who had supported the Allied* cause during World War I, felt betrayed by these underhand tactics. Meanwhile France, in particular, ran its mandates less like developing states and more like nineteenth-century-style colonies. When the two Western powers made a hasty and messy withdrawal from the region a quarter of a century later after the horrors of World War II,* it only complicated relations with the Arab nations further. Then came the declaration in 1948 that the State of Israel was being officially formed; this resulted in a region-wide war and the displacement of millions of Palestinians.

Since these problematic events in modern Arab–Western relations, it has been difficult not to associate the medieval Crusades with this colonial mandate period—and hard to view the Crusades without the swirl of emotions and rhetoric of the twentieth century. By combining the actions of these recent events with those of 800 years ago, the very crux of the postcolonialist* view of the Crusades was created: that the Crusaders were always merciless invaders and the Muslims always helpless victims. Yet Hillenbrand proves that not only were Muslims happy to live under the rule of Crusaders, but that Muslim states actually cooperated with, and even supported, the continued presence of Frankish powers in the Levant. Given the strength of her sources, Hillenbrand's revelations were nothing short of revolutionary.

NOTES

1 See Amin Maalouf, *The Crusades through Arab Eyes* (London: Al Saqi Books, 1984).

2 Carole Hillenbrand, *The Crusades: Islamic Perspectives* (Edinburgh: Edinburgh University Press, 1999), 20.

3 Hillenbrand, *The Crusades,* 365.

SECTION 2
IDEAS

MODULE 5
MAIN IDEAS

KEY POINTS

- Hillenbrand's five themes in *The Crusades* concern Muslim reactions to the First Crusade,* the idea of jihad,* relations between Muslims and Franks,* the detail of Crusading war and warfare, and finally, modern Islamic scholarly views and presentations of the Crusades.*

- She argues that an understanding of the modern Islamic world and its attitudes to the West can be gained from the consideration of historic Islamic perspectives on the Crusades.

- *The Crusades* is the first work to solely use Islamic sources to examine the events of the Crusades, and the only text to do so on such a large scale.

Key Themes

Carole Hillenbrand deals with five themes in *The Crusades: Islamic Perspectives* in an attempt to build a complete picture of the Crusades and contemporaneous life in the Levant* from the viewpoint of the Arabic Muslims who witnessed them.

First, she uses her sources to demonstrate the reaction of contemporary Muslims to the First Crusade and the arrival of the Franks in the Middle East* in 1096–9. She searched widely for evidence in many early histories and previously untranslated or little-known manuscripts, to reveal both continuity and change in the mindset and political landscape of the Muslim Levant. She reveals how the native populations came to terms with the arrival of the alien newcomers. In Hillenbrand's second-themed section, she addresses the presentation of jihad in the Muslim world, in this case referring to

❝ The basic idea of this book is simple: to tell the story of the Crusades as they were seen, lived, and recorded on 'the other side'—in other words, in the Arab camp. **❞**
Amin Maalouf, *The Crusades through Arab Eyes*

the evolution of its meaning from an inner spiritual struggle to fulfil one's faith, to its more modern understanding as a physical struggle against the opponents of Islam.

Contemporary relations between the Franks and Muslims are analyzed within the book's third theme, where Hillenbrand discusses both the various Muslim perceptions of the Crusaders, and Islamic portrayals of daily life in the Holy Land. Her fourth topic comprises a detailed study of Islamic accounts of warfare and other military concerns in the Levant. She addresses depictions of the equipment of war, before considering accounts of wars and campaigns. The book concludes with its fifth theme, as Hillenbrand considers how modern Islamic authors and political and cultural organizations have employed the idea of the Crusades. She ends with a key suggestion—that by considering the Crusades from both medieval and modern Islamic perspectives, we can gain a greater understanding of the modern Islamic world and its attitudes toward the West.

Hillenbrand has one overarching argument in *The Crusades*—that previous histories of the period have missed a large part of the evidence that records the events of that era. As a result, anyone who studied the Crusades had only been given a partial account of the subject. Yet by unearthing so many new and detailed sources, Hillenbrand has been able to create a comprehensive analysis of the Crusades to redress the balance, one that is often contrary to the expectations of modern readers. For example, she disproves the preconception that both sides had nothing but enmity for one another, and the assumption that there was little or no cultural exchange and everyday interaction between the two groups. In this way, Hillenbrand has revealed more information about the daily realities of life for medieval Muslims than had previously been available elsewhere.

Exploring the Ideas

The majority of Hillenbrand's ideas are ultimately very straightforward, with much of her text methodically discussing the various Islamic sources and how they can be used to inform our understanding of the Crusades. In her study of the Muslim reaction to the First Crusade (1096–9), for example, she demonstrates how thoroughly divided the Muslim states were prior to the arrival of the Crusaders. This crucial situation enabled the Crusader states* to easily integrate themselves into the Levant's fractured political situation.[1] She quotes medieval historians such as Abu Shama* of Syria, who chronicled the disunity of the Seljuk* Turks following the death of Sultan Malik-shah in 1092. The intense civil war that followed his death was probably the reason for the First Crusade's success in crossing Asia Minor (modern-day Turkey) in 1097–8. It is worth noting that, although the Crusaders were often called an "Army of God," the massed groups normally included thousands of ordinary (if armed) pilgrims, as well as all the usual civilian camp-followers. With the local populations focused on fighting each other, the Crusaders even reached Syria and Palestine intact, a feat that none of the subsequent Crusades ever managed.

Meanwhile, the leaders of Syria and Egypt were also at loggerheads following the deaths of their own leaders in 1094. This enabled the Crusaders (once they had completed a prolonged but successful siege of Antioch in eastern Syria) to make a dash for Jerusalem unimpeded, leading to their seizure of the Holy City. Ali ibn Al-Athir's* mournful understatement that "the Sultans disagreed ... and the Franks seized their lands"[2] sums up the situation perfectly.

This evidence of severe disunity among the Levant's Muslim powers clearly disproves any arguments that the Islamic world was a tranquil oasis of peace prior to the arrival of the European armies. If anything, the arrival of the Crusaders provided an opportunity for the local elites to make use of the newcomers' military power, by forging new alliances with them. As the chronicler Ibn al-Adim* noted: "The political elite of Aleppo were in favor of the continuing existence of the Franks in Syria, because it helped them to perpetuate the independent status of their city."[3]

Language and Expression

The Crusades is divided into two parts. The first is composed of chronological chapters dealing with the arrival of the First Crusade and the evolution of Muslim thought and responses to the presence and eventual removal of those invaders. The second section studies a range of aspects of Crusade-era life, including ethnic and religious stereotypes, military life, and equipment. To end, Hillenbrand addresses the legacy of the Crusades, in both the modern Islamic world and the West.

As a result, the book is a curious hybrid. At first, it is a straight history, telling a story from beginning to end. Then it switches to a collection of shorter, almost article-like chapters that examine topics as diverse as the cross as a symbol of bad luck, sexual practices, and the lack of hygiene among the Franks. Hillenbrand also discusses other practical issues, such as the language barrier and contemporary medicine—and her sources clearly show that medicine (not to mention hygiene) in the Arab world was vastly superior to that of the Franks.

Meanwhile, the language of the book is rich and expressive, and Hillenbrand's translations of the manuscripts are full of the vigor and spirit of Arabic, without rendering it clichéd or infantile in direct conversion to English. Although the text's format can feel fragmented, as a record of the era from the viewpoint of Arabic Muslims there are few details missing from the picture it paints.

NOTES

1   Carole Hillenbrand, *The Crusades: Islamic Perspectives* (Edinburgh: Edinburgh University Press, 1999), 83–4.

2   Hillenbrand, *The Crusades,* 83.

3   Hillenbrand, *The Crusades,* 83.

MODULE 6
SECONDARY IDEAS

KEY POINTS

- Hillenbrand had five subordinate ideas in *The Crusades*: first, an expanded analysis of Muslim reactions to the First Crusade* of the end of the eleventh century; second, the concept of jihad* as a propaganda* tool; third, cultural interchange from the Islamic societies to the Crusaders; fourth, new concepts in fortification introduced by the Crusaders; and finally, misrepresentation of Islamic sources.

- As with the main ideas of the text, Hillenbrand's subordinate ideas enrich the reader's understanding of the Crusades* and provide a broader perspective than traditional Eurocentric* histories of the same events.

- Hillenbrand's discussion of previously unknown or misrepresented sources has been hugely influential and much discussed.

Other Ideas

Each of the five themes of Carole Hillenbrand's *The Crusades: Islamic Perspectives* contains subordinate concepts that significantly affect major aspects of those principal ideas. For example, she provides original Islamic sources that provide a secondary, groundbreaking subtext to her first main theme—Muslim reactions to the First Crusade. Hillenbrand's previously undiscovered sources reveal that the reactions of locals to the first wave of Crusaders was, on the whole, less extreme than their responses to later Crusades.[1] This hypothesis is at considerable odds with other historical accounts of the period, such as Lebanese historian Amin Maalouf's* *The Crusades through Arab Eyes* (1984).

❝ Too often we rely on literary sources—the writings of philosophers, historians, poets and playwrights as our primary sources ... This has pitfalls. ❞

M. Shahid Alam,* *Racism across Civilizations*

Second, Hillenbrand argues that the presentation of jihad in the twelfth and thirteenth centuries was very much a part of the propaganda machines of the Muslim rulers. The term jihad (when not used to refer to an inner spiritual struggle with one's faith) had originally described a war to convert infidels (unbelievers) to Islam.[2] However, the Arabic empires had become secure following the great Islamic conquests of the seventh and eight centuries, so this idea had largely been allowed to lapse. Yet with the arrival of the Crusaders, it was suddenly necessary for Islamic thinkers to rehabilitate the term in light of the new threat. Therefore "jihad" began to be presented as a defensive war in a wave of new, anti-Crusader propaganda.

Third, she suggests that Muslims of the Middle Ages* did not change their stereotypes of Christianity during the period of the Crusades, continuing to regard Westerners as violent, uneducated barbarians. Nor did they perceive the Catholic* invasions as an equivalent to an Islamic jihad,[3] with most locals assuming this was merely another war, not a religiously motivated campaign.

While there was a great deal of contact between Muslims and Franks,* the cultural influences went predominantly one way—from the Muslim world to the Crusaders.[4] Europe benefited from this renewed contact with the Classical learning that had been preserved by Islamic scholars, notably the works of the influential Greek philosopher Aristotle,* and Arabic scientific advances. The Western adoption of Arabic numerals (1, 2, 3, 4, 5) in place of their cumbersome Roman equivalents (I, II, III, IV,V) was one such lasting benefit.

Fourth, Hillenbrand argues that it was the Franks who led the innovations made in the field of fortification in the Holy Land during this era.[5] It was only when the Arab nations finally learnt to destroy these inventive new fortresses that they were able to remove the Crusaders from the Levant.*[6]

Hillenbrand's fifth point is explored throughout the book. This is the relevance of Islamic sources for the Crusade to the historians and politicians of the modern world. She argues that misunderstandings and misrepresentations of these sources have been a major problem during the past century, leading to the hardening of attitudes, particularly in the Arab world, and unfortunately, continued conflict and human misery.[7]

Exploring the Ideas

Although the majority of ideas contained in Hillenbrand's text are not in themselves original, she investigates them in greater detail than previous studies. *The Crusades* also offers an original perspective, for most of Hillenbrand's sources have never been read before (certainly outside of a small circle of Arab-speaking specialists). As a result, she is able to contribute new material and arguments to narratives that had previously felt well-worn and predictable. For example, her consideration of jihad rhetoric (persuasive language associated with the subject of jihad), explored alongside evidence of peaceful interaction between Christians and Muslims, allows Hillenbrand to argue that relations between Crusaders and Muslims were frequently more complex than has been previously suggested.[8]

In the Islamic view, for example, the Crusades were not initially thought to be any different from other conflicts, either previous or ongoing. Therefore no existing Arabic work from that period concentrates solely on the Crusades. "They are simply wars," Hillenbrand says.[9] The Arab peoples did not put any special significance on the fact that the Crusaders were Christian. After all, both the Arabs and Turks had a long history of relations and conflicts with the Christian Byzantine Empire.* In addition, they had perhaps millions of native Christian subjects living in their own lands. Indeed, Hillenbrand explains that there had been centuries of general tolerance for "People of the Book" in the "House of Islam." The true nature of the Crusades—that they were a holy war intended to break the power of Islamic civilization and restore the borders of the ancient Christian Roman Empire—only slowly dawned on those who were its targets.

Once this connection between the violence of the Franks and their Christian religion had been made, however, local Christians were soon scapegoated as responsible for the violence of their co-religionists. Although Hillenbrand is cautious about attributing truth to accounts that might have been based on exaggeration, she discovers definitive proof that Christians in Aleppo faced reprisals for Frankish raids in the region in 1124.[10] Even today, the fate of Middle Eastern* Christians in times of conflict is regularly overlooked. Thus the examination of their fortunes in the medieval era is another example of Hillenbrand's comprehensive range of ideas and topics.

Overlooked

There is little inside Hillenbrand's text that has been overlooked by her fellow English-speaking historians. On the contrary, *The Crusades* has been hugely influential in the academic field of Crusades studies. The content of the book itself, however, has been somewhat overlooked by the wider audience of academia and political disciplines that might also benefit from its research and reach. In addition to its political and religious themes relating to the Crusading era, Hillenbrand's text provides considerable detail on a number of other topics, such as gender studies, medieval travel, and literature. Despite its reviews mentioning Hillenbrand's coverage of wars, jihad, and fanaticism, *The Crusades* is much more than a chronicle of battles and campaigns. It is, in fact, a repository of information on everyday life during the Crusading period in the months and years between conflicts.

Historians who have accessed the book include the British research fellow Susan Rose;* she has utilized Hillenbrand's lengthy discussion of naval traditions in the period. Also, the Israeli sociologist Tahir Abbas* uses *The Crusades* to draw parallels between the Crusader states* and modern-day Britain, in his study of how different communities can coexist in relative harmony. One of Hillenbrand's sources, which Abbas cites, is the memoir of Usama bin Munqidh,* a Syrian knight in Saladin's* army. Though Usama was an Arab, it seems he had many friends among the Franks, and he writes at length on their differences in culture and habits, often comically. He was constantly amused by Western knights' attempts to ape Arab customs, describing how one Frankish friend only learned to use a public bath in his elder years. Usama's easy contacts with the Catholic knights in Jerusalem proves that his social situation was clearly normal at the time, and he paints an image of a thriving multicultural society that could serve as a model for successful living, even now.

NOTES

1   Carole Hillenbrand, *The Crusades: Islamic Perspectives* (Edinburgh: Edinburgh University Press, 1999), 83–4.

2   Hillenbrand, *The Crusades*, 246–8.

3   Hillenbrand, *The Crusades*, 321–2.

4   Hillenbrand, *The Crusades*, 419–20.

5   Hillenbrand, *The Crusades*, 502–4.

6   Hillenbrand, *The Crusades*, 578–81.

7   Hillenbrand, *The Crusades*, 611–12.

8   Hillenbrand, *The Crusades*, 248.

9   Hillenbrand, *The Crusades*, 9.

10   Hillenbrand, *The Crusades,* 412.

MODULE 7
ACHIEVEMENT

KEY POINTS

- *The Crusades* has significantly widened the base of knowledge that scholars have at their disposal in discussions of the period.

- With her translation of many previously undiscovered or under-examined texts, Hillenbrand has opened the door to a sizable number of "new" sources for scholars throughout the world.

- Hillenbrand has nonetheless been criticized for limiting the sources under examination to Islamic texts only.

Assessing The Argument

Carole Hillenbrand's primary goal when writing *The Crusades: Islamic Perspectives* was to build a thorough history of the Crusades* using a comprehensive collection of rarely seen and relatively unknown Islamic sources. In this, she has been highly successful, aptly illustrating the necessity of including these sources and perspectives when examining the events of the period—although her attempts to bring art and architecture to the heart of Crusades studies have been less fruitful.

The Crusades has had an international impact on subsequent works on the Crusading era, and Hillenbrand has influenced a large number of scholars. Now, with the text serving as a core teaching material at leading British universities such as Cambridge and St. Andrew's, she is guaranteed to influence the next generation of historians.

The usefulness and topicality of *The Crusades* has also been enhanced by recent world events. Holy wars, which were once long

> **❝**Carole has published [*The Crusades*] out of the
> conviction that the best scholarship on Islamic history
> and Islamic studies should view Islam not just as a
> religion but also as a civilization.**❞**
> Yasir Suleiman, ed., *Living Islamic History*

thought extinct in the developed world, have suddenly been brought
sharply back into focus and this has heightened interest in a better
understanding of previous religious conflicts. The ongoing activities
of militant Islamist* terrorist groups—in particular ISIS*/Daesh, al-
Shabaab, and al-Qaeda affiliates—in areas as diverse as the Middle
East,* sub-Saharan Africa, and South Asia as well as ongoing attacks
on the Western world, ensure that this trend will continue. Islamism is
an ideology that advocates the implementation and use of Islamic
religious law throughout all aspects of public and private life.

Criticism of Hillenbrand's work, which has not been extensive, has
largely been directed at the limitations of its sole focus on Islamic
sources from the Levant* region. For example, the text barely
mentions that a similar, concurrent struggle was taking place at the
opposite end of the Mediterranean. In Spain and Portugal, Catholic*
forces were engaged in reconquering these countries from Islamic
forces, a war in which Christian soldiers were promised similar
heavenly rewards to those fighting in the Holy Land; it is worth noting
that this conflict is not now commonly referred to as a "Crusade."

Due to a tight focus on contemporary Islamic sources from the
Levant, the time frame in Hillenbrand's text is also limited to the
Crusaders' first appearances in the region. As result, the book does not
cover any of the usual background to the Crusades, or the earliest
stages of their journey. As Hillenbrand relates, the rulers of Baghdad
only heard about the First Crusade* (launched in 1096) when
refugees arrived after the fall of Jerusalem in 1099.

Achievement in Context

The Crusades has found relevance in two distinct areas. First, since Hillenbrand's work, it has become commonplace for introductory overviews and histories of the Crusades to make extensive use of Islamic sources and perspectives. Two such examples are David Nicolle's* *The Crusades* and Jonathan Phillips's* *The Crusades 1095–1197*,[1] where Phillips refers to Hillenbrand's book as a "landmark work" that allows "a fuller and clearer appreciation of the impact of the Crusades in the Eastern Mediterranean."[2] He also states that Hillenbrand's scholarship has proved essential to understanding certain particularly pivotal issues in European history.[3] He cites as examples Hillenbrand's detailed examination of the relationship between Arabic forces and the sea, and the way she revealed the previously unknown personality of the twelfth-century leader Imad ad-Din Zengi.*[4] Though Zengi's success in bringing about the first major defeat of Crusader forces earned him a hero's reputation, Hillenbrand reveals him to be a tyrannical and reckless despot.

Unsurprisingly, Hillenbrand's work has also had an impact in discussions of terrorism and ongoing relations between the West and the Muslim world, particularly following 9/11* and the ongoing War on Terror.* The historian J. M. B. Porter* cites the authentic medieval Muslim voices in *The Crusades* to refute "recent Muslim—particularly Arab—scholarship which reinterprets the Crusades in light of the nineteenth and twentieth century history of colonialism,* Arab nationalism,* and the creation of the Israeli state."[5]

In Porter's view, *The Crusades* demonstrates that although the events of ten centuries ago share some superficial similarities with the current period—the presence of Western armies and a non-Muslim state in the Eastern Mediterranean region, for example—they cannot be likened to those of the modern era. In consequence he states that any attempts to draw a parallel between the French Catholic-led First Crusade* in 1096–99 and the American-backed declaration of the

State of Israel in 1948 are disingenuous and uninformed. Porter also draws on Hillenbrand's clarifications on the evolution of the term "jihad"* to rebut the common present-day Western assumption that it simply means war against unbelievers, rather than the more subtle and multilayered meanings it holds in reality.

Limitations

Although the global situation (particularly the political situation in the Middle East) has changed greatly since *The Crusades* was published in 1999, these changes have all occurred in the lifetime of today's students and scholars. As a result, Hillenbrand's readers do not need to make particular allowances for any social, temporal, or cultural contexts of the text, and her ideas remain relevant. Nonetheless, in light of these later world events, there are some specific sections that could benefit from revision.

Hillenbrand contextualizes medieval Islamic representations of the Crusades alongside modern political propaganda,* pointing out the major similarities and differences in the observations of an inhabitant of Jerusalem of the eleventh century in comparison with one of the twentieth. Though this remains useful, an updated version could be more relevant to the Muslim world in the aftermath of events such as the American-led invasions of Iraq* in 2003 and Afghanistan* in 2001, and the so-called Arab Spring* (a series of uprisings in the Muslim world, beginning in 2010, that led to new governments in Tunisia, Egypt, Libya, and Yemen). These events have created an even greater need for understanding and communication between Muslims and the West.

Criticism of the text has largely focused on the lack of non-Islamic sources rather than on any culturally specific concerns. Khurram Qadir,* a historian based in Pakistan, has however criticized Hillenbrand's work for its Eurocentric* subject matter—a Christian invasion of the Middle East—and for her general stance. He suggests that "an apologetic view is taken of cases of Christian intolerance and treatment of holy places and then counterbalanced with examples of Muslim intolerance to show this in its true light."[6] This is particularly important because, as Qadir notes: "In [Hillenbrand's] declared intent to 'redress the balance' of a Eurocentric understanding of the [Crusades], the book is not very successful, probably because the author belongs to that tradition of scholarship."[7]

Paul Chevedden,* another scholar of the Crusades, considers the book's start and end points for the Crusades in the eleventh and thirteenth centuries as too limited; for him, they must be viewed as part of a much longer series of interactions and conflicts between Muslims and Christians.[8]

While *The Crusades* has provided new avenues of research for several diverse subjects and hence contributed to the advancement of scholarship in many ways, it is important to note that it is generally used in conjunction with the work of other academics because it only draws on sources relating to one particular religious and ethnic group.

NOTES

1   David Nicolle, *The Crusades* (Oxford: Osprey, 2001); Jonathan Phillips, *The Crusades 1095–1197* (Harlow: Pearson Education, 2002).

2   Phillips, *The Crusades 1095–1197*, 6.

3   Phillips, *The Crusades 1095–1197*, 108.

4   Phillips, *The Crusades 1095–1197*, 48.

5   J. M. B. Porter, "Osama Bin-Laden, *Jihad*, and the Sources of International Terrorism," *Symposium: From Pipe Bombs to PhDs: International Terrorism in the Twenty-First Century, Indiana International and Comparative Law Review* 13 (2002–3): 871–85; and Arie W. Kruglanski and Shira Fishman, "The Psychology of Terrorism: "Syndrome" Versus "Tool" Perspectives," *Terrorism and Political Violence* 18, no. 2 (2006): 193–215.

6   Khurram Qadir, "Modern Historiography: The Relevance of the Crusades," *Islamic Studies* 46, no. 4 (2007): 547–51.

7   Qadir, "Modern Historiography," 551.

8   Paul E. Chevedden, "The Islamic View and the Christian View of the
     Crusades: A New Synthesis," *History* 93, no. 310 (2008): 181–200.

MODULE 8
PLACE IN THE AUTHOR'S WORK

KEY POINTS

- By the time she published *The Crusades*, Hillenbrand had been specializing in non-Western sources for nearly three decades.
- *The Crusades* remains the most ambitious project of her career.
- The book was the result of a lifetime's work in analysis and research across the Middle East.*

Positioning

The Crusades: Islamic Perspectives was published in 1999 at the height of Carole Hillenbrand's career. At the time of its publication she had spent four decades in the study of the Middle Ages* and was a senior member of the department of Islamic and Middle Eastern* studies at the University of Edinburgh, one of the most respected educational institutions in Britain; she would be appointed professor there the following year. The book, the product of a lifetime's work locating and analyzing texts from across the Middle East, is one of the highlights of Hillenbrand's body of work.

Prior to 1999, Hillenbrand wrote a large number and variety of articles relating to the medieval Middle East. In the 1980s, she produced articles in which she made extensive use of Islamic sources in her discussion of the Crusades,* publishing for example "The Establishment of Artuqid* Power in Diyar Bakr in the Twelfth Century," in the Islamic studies journal *Studia Islamica* (1981), and "The Islamic World and the Crusades" in the *Scottish Journal of Religious Studies* in 1987.[1] Her work in the 1990s continued in this vein and considered topics, including Muslim reactions to the First Crusade,*

> **❝ In a long and distinguished career, Carole Hillenbrand has become best known as an Islamic historian of the Seljuks and the Crusades ... However, Carole's scholarly interests go far beyond history in the technical sense to include Sufism* and Islamic thought. ❞**
>
> Yasir Suleiman, ed., *Living Islamic History*

that would be discussed in greater detail in *The Crusades*.[2] In all, she has published more than 60 articles on Islamic history and thought.[3]

While Hillenbrand upheld the main theme of the book in her subsequent works, she moved beyond the narrow focus on Islamic sources that was so strictly adhered to in *The Crusades*. She has considered the role of the Arabic* sources in understanding the Seljuk* invasions of Anatolia,* in conjunction with Byzantine* and Western sources[4] (the Seljuks were a people who migrated from central Asia into Persia in the tenth century, before gradually taking control of surrounding territories; Anatolia, one of these territories, is the Asian portion of modern-day Turkey). Likewise, she has written on the interaction between Islamic and Byzantine sources in the eleventh and twelfth centuries.[5] Her latest work, *Islam: A New Historical Introduction* (2015), is a study of the religion and the civilization that grew up in its wake, each of its chapters examining what is described as a core aspect of the faith—the Prophet Muhammad and the Quran, for example—rather than using a strict chronological form.

Integration

It is unarguable that *The Crusades* represents a peak in Professor Hillenbrand's career. Her undergraduate degree in Somerville College, Oxford focused on Eastern languages and was then rounded with postgraduate study of medieval Arabic* chronicles at the University of Edinburgh.[6] Then, following the completion of her doctorate, Hillenbrand taught and wrote prolifically on Islamic history for two decades, and though some of her publications in that time shifted the focus to medieval civilizations on the periphery of the Muslim world,[7] her academic career has only ever had one direction and all of her papers have been written to look at the medieval world through Islamic eyes.

While Hillenbrand's earlier books, *The Waning of the Umayyad Caliphate* (1987) and *A Muslim Principality in Crusader Times: The Early Artuqid State* (1990), were similar in approach and subject matter to *The Crusades*, both were focused on narrow areas and eras in comparison. She would return to this narrow approach with her fourth book, *Turkish Myth and Muslim Symbol: The Battle of Manzikert** (2007). Her *Islam: A New Historical Introduction* (2015) marked a return to large-scale subject matter, involving analysis of events of historical importance over a period of centuries, as in *The Crusades.*

Each of her publications has revealed something further about the psyche of the greater Islamic civilization throughout the medieval period, a time when it was far and away the most powerful and advanced of the three monotheistic* blocs of Judaism, Christianity, and Islam, ("monothesism" denotes a religion founded on belief in a single deity). The Grand Library of Baghdad, or "House of Wisdom," for example, was the largest in the world before its destruction by the Mongols* in 1258. In shedding light on Islamic views of the Byzantine Empire* or on Muslim rulers' opinions of the nature of the Crusaders' homelands, Hillenbrand has assisted in our understanding of peoples, events, and states that were hitherto either thought to be unknowable or else completely understood and unworthy of serious further study. Without these sources, our understanding of medieval Mediterranean history would remain as blinkered as that of the medieval European scholars themselves.

Significance

The Crusades has been particularly influential among Hillenbrand's body of work, and has been cited extensively, ranging from articles and books on the medieval Middle East, to the work of those investigating social and political trends in the modern world. This influence has been amplified through its translation into other languages, such as Malay and Russian.

Hillenbrand's main achievement is not the originality of the ideas she puts forward, but her willingness to put these ideas into practice, however difficult the circumstances obtaining certain works might be. She has made a considerable contribution to the study of the Crusades through her emphasis on Islamic sources and the analysis of these sources, though it remains to be seen whether *The Crusades* will remain her most important work. Her new history of Islam is arguably even more extensive than her work on the Crusades, so time will tell whether it attains a similar stature. Already, her efforts have formed part of the modern movement in the study of the Crusades in the West, and she has ensured consideration of all sources and perspectives, rather than only those of the Crusaders.

NOTES

1   Carole Hillenbrand, "Some Medieval Islamic Approaches to Source Material," *Oriens* 27/8 (1981): 197–225; Carole Hillenbrand, "The Islamic World and the Crusades," *Scottish Journal of Religious Studies* 8 (1987): 150–57.

2   Carole Hillenbrand, "Aspects of Jihad Propaganda: The Evidence of Twelfth-Century Inscriptions," *Proceedings of the Conference on the History of the Crusades* (Bir Zeit: University of Bir Zeit, 1993), 53–63; Carole Hillenbrand, "The First Crusade: The Muslim Perspective," in *The Origins and Impact of the First Crusade*, ed. J. Phillips (Manchester: Manchester University Press, 1997), 130–41.

3   Thames and Hudson online catalogue information, "Introduction to Islamic Beliefs and Practices in Historical Perspective," accessed October 21, 2015, http://www.thamesandhudsonusa.com/books/introduction-to-islam-beliefs-and-practices-in-historical-perspective-softcover.

4   Carole Hillenbrand, *Turkish Myth and Muslim Symbol: The Battle of Manzikert* (Edinburgh: Edinburgh University Press, 2007).

5   Carole Hillenbrand, "The Arabic Sources," in *The Prosopography of the Byzantine Empire, 1024–1204*, ed. M. Whitby (London: The British Academy, 2007), 283–340.

6   Queen Mary University of London, "Resources for Studying the Crusades," accessed May 30, 2013, http://www.crusaderstudies.org.uk/resources/historians/profiles/hillenbrand/.

7   Carole Hillenbrand, "Some Medieval Muslim Views on Constantinople," in *World Christianity in Muslim Encounter: Essays in Memory of David A. Kerr Vol.2,* ed. Stephen R. Goodwin (London: Continuum, 2009).

SECTION 3
IMPACT

MODULE 9
THE FIRST RESPONSES

KEY POINTS

- The main criticism of *The Crusades* was that it suffered from the limitation of completely ignoring any non-Islamic sources.

- Though Hillenbrand has not addressed this criticism directly, her title and introduction to the text both make it clear that her choice of sources and overall outline were deliberate.

- The ideas and techniques of *The Crusades* were already accepted as being needed by the wider academic world. As a result Hillenbrand's work was widely praised and welcomed.

Criticism

Ironically, given Carole Hillenbrand's intention of remedying the lack of authentic Islamic voices in existing scholarship on Crusades* history by providing a more rounded range of sources from the era, the most common criticism of *The Crusades: Islamic Perspectives* is that it has not provided a sufficient number of sources, and that the inclusion of non–Islamic sources would strengthen the work as a whole.

The work has been criticized in other ways, too. Khurram Qadir,* a key Pakistani scholar of the Crusades, described sections of the work as "meandering" and found fault with some of Hillenbrand's writing and analysis.[1] More significantly, he argued that several areas, such as the chapter on Muslim perceptions of the Franks,* demonstrate personal bias. Among Western scholars of the Crusades, Paul Chevedden* has complained that her work considers the Islamic

> ❝ Essential reading for those who wish to understand not only the past but also the present Middle East, for today the evocation of 'Crusade' is potent propaganda. ❞
>
> Malcolm Barber, Review of *The Crusades: Islamic Perspectives*.

perspective from too narrow a chronological view. Chevedden's contention is that the Norman invasion of Sicily* in 1060 marked the true starting point of the Crusades movement and, as a result, he accuses Hillenbrand of failing "to recognize the Islamic view of the Crusades, because the assumption that forms her starting point is that crusading began in 1095."[2]

Even some of Hillenbrand's supporters have expressed concerns about aspects of her book. In his otherwise positive review, Jonathan Berkey,* an American scholar of medieval Islam, suggests that the "general public" will find her arguments difficult to follow. He maintains that Hillenbrand's narrow focus on the Crusades—rather than a broader consideration of the medieval Middle East*—is detrimental to the study as a whole.[3] Likewise, the Spanish historian Isabel O'Connor* suggests that Hillenbrand's work suffers from its concentration on Islamic sources from the Middle East.[4] Finally, the British scholar of medieval history Malcolm Barber* applauds Hillenbrand's work as an "excellent [book], essential reading for those who wish to understand not only the past but also the present Middle East"—but also criticizes Hillenbrand's claim to be the first author to put greater emphasis on non-Western sources and perspectives.[5]

It is worth noting that much of the criticism of Hillenbrand's work has appeared in review articles, where academic convention obliges the authors to locate and expose weaknesses in any work they review. As a result, criticism in this format is typically tempered with overall praise, and Hillenbrand's text has generally been viewed as a valuable addition to the existing scholarship. Other historians and academics, such as J. M. B. Porter,* Susan Rose,* Arie Kruglanski* and Shira Fishman,* have identified the text's strengths and made use of them in their work.[6]

Responses

In the introduction to the book, Hillenbrand preemptively addressed potential criticisms, stating that "as a pioneering venture, [*The Crusades*] cannot hope to do more than sketch an outline for future research."[7] Since then, she has not responded directly to any criticism of her work, though the 2006 edition of the book does go further in both explaining her rationale for its structure, and examining the transformed climate of Crusader scholarship in the wake of 9/11* and the (then-ongoing) Iraq War.* Her subsequent works have used a broader range of source materials, which could be seen as a reaction to the criticism of *The Crusades'* restricted field of reference. It is more likely, however, that Hillenbrand has simply returned to the style of academic study seen in her previous works, where she has explored all available texts relating to her subject.

A further important criticism of Hillenbrand's work is that it fails to provide an account of the Crusades that is accessible to students with little prior knowledge of the period. The root of this problem is Hillenbrand's narrow approach, for by only using Islamic sources from the Levant* region, she has chosen not to cover events that took place before the Crusaders arrived, nor events that took place in other geographical areas. As a result, a true overview and understanding of the Crusading era can only be reached by reading other histories in conjunction with *The Crusades.* This is another area of criticism that has not been addressed by Hillenbrand.

Conflict and Consensus

There has not been a great debate over Hillenbrand's work, for while there are criticisms that focus on the text's limitations, even her critics recognize that *The Crusades* is of great value to the current study of the era. Despite the fact that her selection of sources is (deliberately) limited, many of those sources were previously inaccessible, little known, or previously undiscovered. There has also been minimal critical dialogue between Hillenbrand and her critics—but this does not mean that her critics' complaints are unfounded. Her work is indeed very narrow in its focus. For instance, it could be said that any history of the Crusades that omits Pope Urban II's* address in the city of Clermont* in France (where the Pope, the head of the Catholic* Church, summoned Western Catholics to arm themselves and reclaim the city of Jerusalem from Muslim control) is no Crusade history at all. Ignoring the Western portions of Crusader history creates just the sort of limited volume that Hillenbrand intended to transcend with her own work. Two academic wrongs, it could be argued, do not make a right, and Hillenbrand's acknowledgement of these issues does not resolve them. As such, her work would benefit from a broader range of sources, including those from non-Islamic traditions, and also Islamic traditions that are geographically or chronologically removed from the Middle East of the eleventh and twelfth century.

Further, Hillenbrand has not addressed the important claim that the book fails to provide an understandable and accessible account of the Crusades for students with little previous knowledge of the period. It is unlikely that this situation will change. Readers who are new to the topic will still be required to read additional historical volumes in order to complete their understanding of the events and concepts under discussion, and *The Crusades* will remain a valuable resource rather than the final word on the subject.

NOTES

1 Khurram Qadir, "Modern Historiography: The Relevance of the Crusades," *Islamic Studies* 46, no. 4 (2007): 547–51.

2 Paul E. Chevedden, "The Islamic View and the Christian View of the Crusades: A New Synthesis," *History* 93, no. 310 (2008): 181–200.

3 Jonathan P. Berkey, "Review of *The Crusades: Islamic Perspectives*," *International Journal of Middle East Studies* 34, no. 1 (2002): 129 31.

4 Isabel O'Connor, "Review of *The Crusades: Islamic Perspectives*," *Islamic Studies* 42, no. 2 (2003): 357–8.

5 Malcolm Barber, "Review of *The Crusades: Islamic Perspectives*," *History Today* (2000), accessed December 10, 2015, http://www.historytoday.com/malcolm-barber/crusades-islamic-perspectives.

6 See J. M. B. Porter, "Osama Bin-Laden, *Jihad*, and the Sources of International Terrorism," *Symposium: From Pipe Bombs to PhDs: International Terrorism in the Twenty-First Century, Indiana International and Comparative Law Review* 13 (2002–3): 871–85; Susan Rose, *Medieval Naval Warfare, 1000–1500* (London: Routledge, 2002), 21, 36; and Arie W. Kruglanski and Shira Fishman, "The Psychology of Terrorism: 'Syndrome' Versus 'Tool' Perspectives," *Terrorism and Political Violence* 18, no. 2 (2006): 207.

7 Carole Hillenbrand, *The Crusades: Islamic Perspectives* (Edinburgh: Edinburgh University Press, 1999), 1.

MODULE 10
THE EVOLVING DEBATE

KEY POINTS

- Following the publication of *The Crusades* in 1999, other more general histories of the Crusades* began to include non-Western sources.

- In the years since Hillenbrand's work, the notion of including Islamic and other non-Western sources has become more popular across studies of the medieval world in general.

- The influence of *The Crusades* has been seen in the English-speaking world. Yet due to the lack of an Arabic* translation, this success has not been replicated in the Islamic world.

Uses And Problems

Carole Hillenbrand's *The Crusades: Islamic Perspectives* is particularly relevant today, given the near-perpetual crisis engulfing the Middle East.* When in 2002 George W. Bush,* the president of the United States, made the controversial decision to describe his policies in the region as a "Crusade," it was symptomatic of the ignorance of the past that Hillenbrand was trying to counter in *The Crusades.* Bush followed this with other, potentially even more explosive, statements and actions that only exacerbated his use of the word. Meanwhile, following the train bombings by politically radicalized Islamic terrorists in Madrid* in 2004, Spain's prime minister, Jose Maria Aznar,* stated that Spain's conflict with the fundamental Islamist* group al-Qaeda* began not in the twenty-first century but in the eighth—thereby linking the phenomenon of modern Islamism (the political ideology of these terrorists) with Spain's history as part of the Islamic empire.

66 More than 30 years ago (1978) when I first traveled
to Indonesia the Crusades were decidedly *not* relevant
... In the early years of the twenty-first century it is a
salient term in Muslim discourse. **99**

Mark Woodward,* *Tropes of the Crusades in Indonesian Muslim
Discourse*

The British author Giles Tremlett* has noted that Osama bin
Laden,* the mastermind of the 9/11* terrorist attacks,[1] had previously
stated the same belief as Aznar. Indeed, comments like those of Bush
and Aznar unfortunately play into the hands of terrorists, whose tactic
is to use the historical violence of the Crusades to stoke present-day
violence and sectarianism across the Middle East and throughout the
world.

Academically, *The Crusades* has played a key part in the evolution
of Crusades studies, a field that has grown exponentially in recent
years. Subsequent authors on the era have frequently cited
Hillenbrand's work, and it is possible to identify a series of studies of
the Crusades that have built on Hillenbrand's themes—the British
historian Jonathan Riley-Smith's* *The Crusades, Christianity and Islam*
(2008) is one particularly noteworthy example.[2] In this work, Riley-
Smith makes extensive use of contemporary Islamic sources and
creates connections between the Crusades and the modern political
climate. Just as his earlier works had influenced Hillenbrand, it is clear
Riley-Smith has now been influenced by her text in turn.

Schools of Thought

The ideas Hillenbrand presents in *The Crusades* have made connections
with a great many scholars and academics. In 2010, Edinburgh
University Press published a volume of essays titled *Living Islamic
History: Studies in Honour of Professor Carole Hillenbrand*. In his preface,

its editor, the renowned scholar Yasir Suleiman,* restates *The Crusades'* core idea:"The best scholarship on Islamic History and Islamic Studies should view Islam not just as a religion but also as a civilization."[3] Suleiman's own contribution is an essay exploring the links between nationalism and poetry, which echoes Hillenbrand's own tendency to examine history outside of more traditional sources such as written chronicles.

Hillenbrand's ideas about the use of non-Western sources and the reality of life in the Crusader states* have been applied to a wide array of topics in the study of the medieval Middle East, by a range of thinkers from the broader postcolonial* school. Her attempt to introduce a better understanding of the Crusades into the modern political arena has been continued by several authors, in light of recent developments in the Middle East. This has become particularly relevant in light of public debates on the meaning of the term "jihad"* and the significance of the Crusades* with reference to 9/11, the wars in Afghanistan* and Iraq,* and ongoing conflicts and terrorist attacks.[4] The ideas Hillenbrand presents now constitute an important basis for much modern scholarship related to the Crusades. Although her influence and that of associated authors has not been revolutionary, it has certainly contributed to the dominant methodology used by Crusade scholars in the West today.

In Current Scholarship

The proponents of Hillenbrand's *The Crusades* are predominantly Western scholars of the Crusades who have, in the main, agreed with her core idea of making greater use of Islamic sources in their studies. After all, this fits well with current trends in Western academia, including recent attempts at greater understanding of other cultures and a movement away from Eurocentrism.* While Hillenbrand's work is most often used as a reference text, due to the sources on which she draws, the widespread use of *The Crusades* shows an implicit acceptance of her idea that Arabic sources are vital to the full understanding of Crusades history.

Hillenbrand's text is important to many academics. It serves as an introduction to Islamic perspectives for students, as well as a reference guide to the works of more established scholars, such as British historian Christopher Tyerman's* *God's War: A New History of the Crusades* (2007). Her ideas have also been applied in associated fields, such as comparing the use of Islamic sources from before and after the Crusading era, and the use of other underrepresented sources from distinct cultural and religious groups.

The intellectual movement of postcolonialism and its focus on the various cultural and linguistic legacies of the colonial period, with which Hillenbrand is connected, is influential in Western study of the Crusades and the medieval Muslim world. However, while scholars have been increasingly prepared to employ a broader range of viewpoints, Hillenbrand's scholarly movement has had less influence on popular representations of the Crusades. In wider Western society, a generally Eurocentric and confrontational image of the period remains the common assumption.

Likewise, Hillenbrand's school has had little impact in the Muslim world for practical reasons—the lack of an Arabic translation has meant that the majority of her sources, though originally written in Arabic, have still not been published for a mass audience and remain obscure.

NOTES

1   Giles Tremlett, *Ghosts of Spain* (London: Faber and Faber, 2006).

2   Jonathan Riley-Smith, *The Crusades, Christianity and Islam* (New York: Columbia University Press, 2008).

3   Yasir Suleiman, ed., *Living Islamic History: Studies in Honour of Professor Carole Hillenbrand* (Edinburgh: Edinburgh University Press, 2010), xiii.

4   J. M. B. Porter, "Osama Bin-Laden, *Jihad*, and the Sources of International Terrorism," *Symposium: From Pipe Bombs to PhDs: International Terrorism in the Twenty-First Century, Indiana International and Comparative Law Review* 13 (2002–3): 871–5; Arie W. Kruglanski and Shira Fishman, "The Psychology of Terrorism: "Syndrome" Versus "Tool" Perspectives," *Terrorism and Political Violence* 18.2 (2006): 193–215.

MODULE 11
IMPACT AND INFLUENCE TODAY

KEY POINTS

- *The Crusades* remains an important and relevant text today, as no other historian in the field of Crusades* studies (including Hillenbrand herself) has published a work matching its scope and ambition.

- Certain sections of Hillenbrand's text remain contentious, particularly in the Middle East,* where her findings directly challenge the traditional narrative of the Crusading period.

- In countries where it has been translated into the native language, *The Crusades* has formed an alternate viewpoint to the prevailing schools of anti-colonialism.*

Position

Although more recent works have provided better overall introductions to the Crusades, or a broader analysis using a combination of both Western and Islamic sources, Carole Hillenbrand's *The Crusades: Islamic Perspectives* remains the only point of reference where students and scholars can access so many underutilized Islamic texts. Indeed, due to her range of materials, Hillenbrand's work has directly influenced the authors of these new introductions to the Crusades, such as the British historians Christopher Tyerman* and Jonathan Phillips.* In this way, she has indirectly influenced their many readers in turn.[1]

With events in the former Crusader states* of the Middle East making international headlines on an almost daily basis, debates on the Crusades have become increasingly topical, which has enhanced the usefulness of Hillenbrand's text in current academia. While there has been debate about the limitations created by her sole inclusion of

> **❝** The Crusader State, re-conquered by the Muslims after centuries, often is invoked as a parallel to contemporary jihad in showing proof of success. **❞**
>
> Arie W. Kruglanski* and Shira Fishman,* *The Psychology of Terrorism: " Syndrome" Versus "Tool" Perspectives*

Islamic sources, this restricted scope has not undermined the value of the text as a work of reference.

Hillenbrand's book has also made an impact beyond discussions of the Crusades themselves and, indeed, the medieval period in general. In addition to being cited in fields as diverse as racism,[2] teaching,[3] and medicine,[4] *The Crusades* has had an impact on the discussion of terrorism and relations between the West and Muslim world, and it will continue to do so for the foreseeable future.[5]

Interaction

The text still challenges contemporary thinkers and schools of thought. For example, Western readers may be surprised by the relative lack of prominence of Saladin* in Hillenbrand's Islamic sources, where he is treated as merely one among many champions of the faith and is not described in the near-worshipful terms that Western histories tend to employ.

More particularly, the core ideas of Hillenbrand's work are at odds with much of the scholarship produced within the Middle East in relation to the Crusades (for example, by proving frequent periods of peaceful coexistence between Crusaders and Muslims) and also contradict a proportion of popular history produced in the West in recent years. Among the Middle Eastern texts challenged by Hillenbrand is Fayid Hammad Muhammad 'Ashur's* *Islamic Jihad against the Crusaders and Mongols in the Mamluk Period* (1995).[6] This text is permeated with an overt political agenda and an inclination toward moralizing, and Hillenbrand argues that works such as 'Ashur's are designed "not to give a scholarly historical account of his subject" but instead to create "a rallying cry for jihad* against present-day governments in the Middle East."[7]

In sharp contrast to more propagandist authors who still tend to focus their arguments and analysis on the narrow range of sources that suit their purposes, Hillenbrand emphasizes the need to include and understand a wide range of Islamic texts. Yet she cannot claim to have been particularly successful: numerous scholars still exist, in the Western and Muslim academic worlds, who do not make full use of the available source materials.

Perhaps the political turmoil that has existed since *The Crusades* was published has contributed to its failure to overcome these hurdles. Events such as 9/11,* the so-called War on Terror,* the 2004 Islamist* bomb attacks in Madrid,* the 2005 London* bombings, the 2015 terror attacks on Paris,* along with many other terrorist atrocities worldwide, have raised tensions between the West and the Muslim world. This has sadly hindered the interaction of academic communities, and despite the attempts at scholarly amalgamation made by Hillenbrand, the arguments and views presented by statesmen and scholars alike in the West and Middle East have often become more polarized. For example, Jum'ah Muhammad Mustafá Jindi's* *Crusader Colonization in Palestine* (2006), a major work by an Islamic scholar, makes no reference to Hillenbrand or any work produced in the West after the 1970s.[8]

The Continuing Debate

The Crusades remains a significant part of current intellectual debate in Western scholarship on the Crusades, serving both as a reference tool and an influence for students and scholars researching the topic. While there have been criticisms of some of Hillenbrand's intellectual arguments, her book is mostly challenging to those scholars who place emphasis on a restricted group of texts in order to further their own analysis. This includes those in the West, such as the British historian Steven Runciman,* who take a firmly Eurocentric* view of the Crusades.

In the few places in the Muslim world where *The Crusades* has been accessible, it has formed a counter to doctrines of anti-colonialism.*[9] However, responses to Hillenbrand's text by Islamic academics have been limited and uncoordinated. This could be due in large part to the difficulties that exist in obtaining access to the work, which has not been translated into Arabic. In fact, the majority of authors who would be most challenged by Hillenbrand's arguments have either not been able to read the book, remain ignorant of its existence, or have simply not troubled to comment on its arguments.

Finally, the political consequences of the arguments that Hillenbrand presents mean that political concerns will always play a role in discussion of the text. In today's highly volatile climate with regard to religion and foreign policy, particularly in the Middle East, the removal of modern politics from the discussion of the Crusades is practically impossible. The story of medieval Islam's cooperation with, opposition to, and ultimate destruction of the Crusader states* resonates as much today as it did immediately after 9/11. For as long as these events continue to influence political and religious discussion, *The Crusades'* utility as a key to understanding them will continue.

NOTES

1   Jonathan Phillips, *The Crusades 1095–1197* (Harlow: Pearson Education, 2002), xi.

2   M. Shahid Alam et al., "Eurocentrism, Sinocentrism and World History: A Symposium," *Science & Society* 67, no. 2 (Summer 2003): 173–217.

3   Dawn Marie Hayes, "Harnessing the Potential in Historiography and Popular Culture When Teaching the Crusades," *The History Teacher* 40, no. 3 (2007): 349–61.

4   Harry Brewer, "Historical Perspectives on Health: Early Arabic Medicine," *The Journal of the Royal Society for the Promotion of Health* 124.4 (2004): 184–7.

5   J. M. B. Porter, "Osama Bin-Laden, *Jihad*, and the Sources of International Terrorism," *Symposium: From Pipe Bombs to PhDs: International Terrorism in the Twenty-First Century, Indiana International and Comparative Law Review* 13 (2002–3): 871–85

6   F. H. M. 'Ashur, *Al-jihad al-islami didd al-salibiyyan wa'l-murghul fi'l-'asr al-mamluk* (Islamic jihad against the Crusaders and Mongols in the Mamluk period) (Tripoli, Lebanon: Jros Press, 1995).

7   Carole Hillenbrand, *The Crusades: Islamic Perspectives* (Edinburgh: Edinburgh University Press, 1999), 4.

8   Jum'ah Muhammad Mustafá Jindi, *Al-istitan al-salibi fi Filastin: 492–690 H./ 1099–1291 M.* (Crusader colonization in Palestine: 492–690AH / 1099–1291CE) (Cairo: Maktabat al-Anjulu al-Misriyah, 2006).

9   Mark Woodward, "Tropes of the Crusades in Indonesian Muslim Discourse," *Contemporary Islam* 4, no. 3 (2010): 311–30.

MODULE 12
WHERE NEXT?

KEY POINTS

- *The Crusades* will most likely remain an important text in the coming years, due to the ongoing topicality of the Middle East* and the Crusades.*

- Its relevance will also be maintained by Hillenbrand's continued work in the field, and the fact that no text as comprehensive has emerged in the decade and a half since publication.

- *The Crusades* is a seminal work that reveals previously unknown aspects of the Crusades due to the extent of its content and the inclusion of many previously undiscussed sources.

Potential

The continuing civil war in Syria and the public emergence of the terror group the Islamic State of Iraq and Syria* (ISIS) in 2014–15 means that, in the foreseeable future, Middle Eastern and Islamic issues will continue to be an important topic in international discourse and politics—even more so than it was when Carole Hillenbrand wrote *The Crusades: Islamic Perspectives.*

Western governments have been considering intervention in these areas for some time, and the terrorist groups have responded to these prospective actions by relying on Crusader imagery to raise local and international support against the West. They openly refer to Western armies, governments, civilians, and even local Iraqi and Syrian forces, as "Crusaders." Meanwhile, in early 2015 the American president, Barack Obama, explicitly compared the religious violence of ISIS with that committed during the First Crusade.*[1] This all proves that,

> ❝ We cannot hope to comprehend—and thereby confront—those who hate us so much unless we understand how they are thinking ... this involves opening our eyes to the actuality ... of our own past. ❞
>
> Jonathan Riley-Smith,* *The Crusades, Christianity and Islam*

since *The Crusades* was published in 1999, the need for a reappraisal of Muslim (and Western) attitudes to the Crusades not only remains but has grown exponentially.

Since the publication of Hillenbrand's work, more academic texts have been written, such as those by historians Niall Christie* and Paul Cobb,[2] that examine the Crusades through the perspective of the Levant's* Muslim inhabitants. Nevertheless, *The Crusades* remains one of the most extensive explorations of the Islamic sources available to modern scholars. Hillenbrand's work is likely to remain as influential until an academic sharing her range of languages and scholarship can write a more complete study.

The idea that Muslim perspectives should be given greater weight in the study of the Crusades will certainly be further developed by modern and future scholars. There are already suggestions that this technique could be applied to studies of interaction between medieval Muslims and Christians in other regions, such as the Iberian* Peninsula in Western Europe. Other authors have suggested using Hillenbrand's method to examine relations between Muslims and Christians prior to the Crusades.

Finally, Hillenbrand's core idea may be expanded by seeking underused sources from yet other perspectives to describe the Crusades. Hillenbrand herself has noted that there is a need to consider the era from the point of view of the Levant's Christians and Jews, and to examine views of the Crusades in the Byzantine* and Armenian* regions. Steps toward introducing these views into Western Crusades scholarship have already been taken and this approach is likely to grow in importance in the future.

Future Directions

In the years since Hillenbrand's work, several introductory overviews of the Crusades have been published that make extensive use of Islamic sources. The British military historian David Nicolle's* *The Crusades* (2001) and Jonathan Phillips's* *The Crusades 1095–1197* (2002) both provide an easier and broader introduction to the Crusades, using sources from outside the Islamic world to provide analyses that cannot be found in Hillenbrand's text.

However, Niall Christie's* *Muslims and Crusaders: Christianity's Wars in the Middle East, 1095–1382, from the Islamic Sources* (2014) is perhaps the closest scholarly work to adhere to—and attempt to build on—Hillenbrand's philosophy and approach. Like Hillenbrand, Christie does not focus solely on battles and wars. Instead he mainly concentrates on the personal and trade relations between the various groups in the Levant at that time, seeking out the apparent incidentals to make a much more rounded history of the period. As a result he also breaks with the more traditionalist views of the Crusades.

To date, Hillenbrand's work has been most influential in the West, but the impact of her ideas may yet grow in the Muslim world and its academic communities. She has already attempted a dialogue with Muslim scholars[3] and a translation of Hillenbrand's work into Malay has made an impact on scholarship in Indonesia.[4] Should this text be translated into Arabic,* it could benefit Middle Eastern affairs by stimulating greater discussion between the Muslim and Western scholarly communities. This would be an outstanding achievement.

Summary

The Crusades is an important work not only because of its core idea—that contemporary Muslim voices must be heard when considering the Crusades—but because of Hillenbrand's success in making this possible. By locating, translating, and analyzing a truly massive range of medieval Islamic texts, she goes far beyond any of her academic predecessors to further our understanding of the Crusades from the Muslim perspective. She even offers new evidence to confound previous assumptions about the era, revealing (for example) how warfare was endemic in the Islamic world even before the Crusaders arrived, and that Muslim society then linked "jihad" to a peaceful inner struggle, not the violence and warfare that Islamist extremism has caused it to be associated with so often today.

Hillenbrand's text is also significant for its attempts to introduce art and architecture as important sources when studying the Crusades, and for its concern with the connections between Crusades studies and the politics of the modern world.

The book is likely to remain important in academic circles for several reasons. For one thing, Hillenbrand herself continues to be an active and significant figure in Crusades studies. It is also unlikely that a more comprehensive study of the Islamic sources will be created in the near future. Furthermore, since the book's publication, increased interest in the Crusades due to ongoing political concerns and world events means that Hillenbrand's ideas have gained even greater importance and topicality in the wider world, as well as in academia. It is Professor Hillenbrand's achievement in accessing and analyzing a range of previously underused sources that gives *The Crusades* its originality and its place as both a key research text and a stellar example of source analysis.

NOTES

1 Evan Simon, "Historians Weigh in on Obama's Comparison of ISIS Militants to Medieval Christian Crusaders," ABC News, February 6, 2015, accessed December 8, 2015, http://abcnews.go.com/Politics/historians-weigh-obamas-comparison-isis-militants-medieval-christian/story?id=28787194.

2 Paul M. Cobb, *The Race for Paradise: An Islamic History of the Crusades*, (Oxford: Oxford University Press, 2014).

3 Carole Hillenbrand, *The Crusades: Islamic Perspectives*, (Edinburgh: Edinburgh University Press, 1999), 5.

4 Mark Woodward, "Tropes of the Crusades in Indonesian Muslim Discourse," *Contemporary Islam* 4, no. 3 (2010): 311–30.

GLOSSARY

GLOSSARY OF TERMS

9/11: a series of attacks made on September 11, 2001, against the United States of America by the Islamist terrorist organization al-Qaeda. Three hijacked passenger aircrafts were crashed into the twin towers of the World Trade Center in New York, and the Pentagon in Virginia. A fourth hijacked aircraft targeted the capital Washington DC, but crashed after its passengers attempted to overpower the hijackers. The 9/11 attacks killed 2,996 people.

Afghanistan War: the ongoing military intervention that began in 2001 by the North Atlantic Treaty Organization (NATO) and allied forces, following the 9/11 attacks on America.

Al-Qaeda: a militant Islamic fundamentalist group that carried out the terrorist attacks against America on September 11, 2001.

Allied forces: an alliance between Britain, France, Russia, and the United States during World War I.

Anatolia: the Asian portion of modern-day Turkey. During the Middle Ages, the region was contested between the Christian Byzantine Empire and a succession of Muslim states, comprising the Umayyad Caliphate, Abbasid Caliphate, Seljuk Turks, and finally the Ottoman Turks.

Anti-colonialism: a term used to describe the opposition to the tenets and practices of colonialism in any form.

Arab nationalism: a nationalist ideology that emphasizes the achievements of Arab civilization and encourages the cultural renewal and political independence and union of Arab societies.

Arab Spring: a term widely used in the media to describe a series of anti-government uprisings in the Muslim world, beginning in 2010. They have led to changes of ruler in Tunisia, Egypt, Libya, and Yemen.

Arabic: the dominant written language of the Muslim Middle East during the Crusades. Most surviving documents from this period were written in Arabic. The language remains dominant in large areas of the modern Middle East and North Africa.

Armenia: most Armenians in the Crusading period lived in the Christian Byzantine Empire in the area that corresponds to eastern Turkey. The Armenian kingdom of Cilicia was established in the late eleventh century in the south of modern Turkey. This kingdom played an important role in the politics of the Crusader states, Byzantium, and local Muslim states.

Artuqid dynasty: a dynasty that ruled Northern Iraq, Northern Syria, and Eastern Turkey during the eleventh and twelfth centuries. They were pivotal in the conflict between the Islamic ruler Saladin and the Seljuk Turks. The dynasty was eventually destroyed by the Seljuks, with the remaining population being absorbed into rival Muslim states.

Byzantine Empire: an extremely powerful empire of Eastern Christians that had initially formed part of the Roman Empire. The Byzantine, or Eastern Roman Empire as it is also known, survived the fall of the Western Roman Empire in the fifth century and continued to dominate the region for another thousand years. The Byzantines were engaged in a series of conflicts with various Muslim states and initially invited, and welcomed, the Catholic Crusaders. But they later came into conflict with the Catholic invaders after their own territories were also looted by Crusaders.

Catholic: originating from the Greek word for "universal," Catholic today refers to the Roman Catholic Church (the largest single domination faith in the world), its followers, and its spiritual leader, the Pope.

Clermont: the French city that hosted the Ecumenical Council called by Pope Urban II in 1095 (that is, a solemn assembly in the Roman Catholic Church, called by the pope, where the pope's decrees become binding.) It is said that Urban preached for knights and great men of France to travel to the East in an armed Crusade, to regain Jerusalem from Muslim control. Urban promised that each Crusader who reached Jerusalem would be granted salvation from sin. His call was highly successful and led to the First Crusade.

Colonialism: generally refers to the exploitation and conquest of much of the world by European powers between the sixteenth and twentieth centuries. The term "colonial" is often used to describe Western intervention in the modern world, and scholarship and opinions that are Eurocentric in nature.

Crusades: a series of religiously motivated invasions of the Levant by Catholics from Western Europe between 1095–6 and 1291. The Crusades began in 1095, after the Byzantine Empire, a Christian kingdom in the Middle East, was invaded by (Muslim) Seljuk Turks. The Byzantine Emperor appealed to the Catholic Pope, Urban II, for assistance. Urban saw an opportunity to reunite the Catholic Church and the Eastern Christians, and reclaim the holy city of Jerusalem from Muslim control. He urged Western Catholics to wage an "armed pilgrimage," offering absolution from sin as a reward. Tens of thousands of armed Catholics reclaimed or seized large areas from the Muslims, including Jerusalem, and established "Crusader states" to govern them.

For two centuries, Western Catholics constantly joined the Crusade, with a larger campaign taking place around once a generation. After the Crusades ended in 1291, the Crusader states were gradually reclaimed. Some broader definitions of the Crusades have been suggested to include holy wars against Muslims in other areas or time periods.

Crusader states: following the success of the First Crusade, a number of Catholic Latin "Crusader states" were established in the Levant after the capture of Jerusalem and defeat of Egyptian forces in 1099. These lands were divided among certain leaders of the Crusade and correspond roughly to the modern countries of Israel/Palestine, Lebanon, and eastern Syria. The largest of these was the Kingdom of Jerusalem.

Eurocentrism: a position that takes a historical and cultural perspective of the world based primarily or solely on Western viewpoints. This was the norm in Western scholarship until around the middle of the twentieth century. Even today, Western academics and politicians are often accused of adopting Eurocentric positions.

First Crusade: a massive, religiously motivated, military invasion of the Levant by Catholic Christians from across Western Europe between 1096 and 1099. The most successful of all the Crusades from a military perspective, the First Crusade resulted in the establishment of the Crusader states in the Levant.

Franks: although this can refer to an early Germanic tribal group, in Crusades studies, Franks generally describes the Crusaders in general, rather than any specific nationality. Many of the Crusaders were from France (Francia).

Greco–Persian Wars: a series of conflicts that ran from roughly 499 to the 330s B.C.E.. Subsequent Greek and Western histories portrayed them as a struggle between Western democracy and Eastern despotism.

Historiography: both the practice and the aims and methods of writing history.

Iberia: a southwestern European peninsula that is today divided between Spain and Portugal, with the British protectorate of Gibraltar in the extreme south.

Imperialism: traditionally referred to the Western military, political, and economic dominance of other areas of the world. In the modern world, the term usually carries negative connotations and is used to criticize Western interference in the rest of the world.

Intifada: a term used to describe an uprising, most often when referring to periods of concerted Palestinian resistance to Israeli rule and occupation. The Second Intifada describes an ongoing, intense Palestinian-Israeli conflict that started with a Palestinian uprising in September 2000.

Iraq War: was fought primarily by a United States-led coalition against Iraq from 2003 to 2011, and led to the deposing of the Iraqi dictator Saddam Hussein. Coalition forces occupied Iraq until 2011, during which time they fought a sporadic insurgency.

Islamic State of Iraq and Syria (ISIS): also known as ISIL and Daesh, a radical Islamist militant group that seized control of large swathes of territory in Iraq and Syria in 2014, and is also known to operate in eastern Libya, the Sinai Peninsula of Egypt, and other areas of the Middle East and North Africa. They have also claimed responsibility for multiple terrorist attacks across the world.

Islamism/Islamist: an ideology that advocates the implementation and use of Islamic religious law throughout all aspects of public and private life.

Jihad: in the context of the Crusades (and modern conflict), this almost invariably refers to "lesser jihad," the physical struggle against opponents of Islam. During the Crusading period, jihad was seen as a defensive holy war to reclaim the Holy Land from the invading Crusaders. However the "greater jihad" describes the inner spiritual struggle in every believer to fulfil his religious duties.

King Faisal International Prize in Islamic Studies: a prestigious award donated by the King Faisal Foundation in Saudi Arabia. The award aims to support and encourage research and to serve Islamic civilization.

Kitab al-Jihad: also known as the *Book of Struggle*, was a treatise published in 1105 by the Damascene writer Ali ibn Tahir al-Sulami. It called for a coordinated, religiously minded resistance to the Christian Crusaders who had arrived in the Levant just over five years before.

League of Nations: an international body established in 1920 by the victorious powers in the wake of World War I to arbitrate international disputes and prevent the reoccurrence of another war between the "Great Powers." It was replaced by the United Nations in 1945.

Levant: a vaguely defined historical geographic region to the east of the Mediterranean. It consists primarily of modern-day Syria, Lebanon, Israel, Jordan, and the Palestinian Territories. However, Cyprus, Iraq, Turkey, and Egypt are sometimes included in this region.

London bombings: a series of coordinated bombings set off by Islamic radicals on the transport network of the British capital on July 7, 2005, killing 52 people.

Madrid bombings: a series of simultaneous bombings set off on the Spanish capital's train system by al-Qaeda on March 11, 2004, killing 191 people.

Mandate: the name given to countries that were placed under the governorship of another country following World War I by the League of Nations. In theory, these countries were independent entities, but de facto were imperial possessions of their steward countries.

Manzikert: a battle fought in 1071 between the forces of the Byzantine Empire (under Emperor Romanos IV Diogenes) and the Seljuk Turks (under Alp Arslan) in eastern Anatolia. The defeat of the Byzantines and the capture of Emperor Romanos led to civil war in the empire and the conquest of much of modern Turkey by the Seljuks.

Middle Ages: a classification used to denote the period between the fall of the Roman Empire in Western Europe (traditionally given as 476) and the European Renaissance in and around 1350.

Middle East: a geographic region roughly containing modern Turkey, Lebanon, Syria, Israel, the Palestinian Territories, Egypt, the Arabian Peninsula, Jordan, Iraq, and Iran.

Mongols: a nomadic, central Asian people who established a Eurasian empire in the thirteenth century.

Monotheism: The belief in one god or deity, from the Greek *mono,* meaning one, and *theos,* meaning god. The first major monotheistic religion was Judaism, and today its two descendent faiths, Christianity and Islam, are the world's largest.

Order of the British Empire (OBE): a title awarded by the British monarch, on the advice of the British government, in recognition of achievements in the arts, sciences, and charities.

Orientalism: broadly describes Western interest in oriental themes. In 1978 Edward Said's book *Orientalism* criticized the Eurocentric attitudes revealed by Western scholars when describing the rest of the world. Since the publication of Said's work, the term "orientalism" has become associated with a patronising attitude among Western scholars toward the rest of the world.

Paris terror attacks: an orchestrated series of terrorist attacks occurring across the French capital on the night of November 13, 2015. In all, 130 people were murdered, with the most deadly assault claiming 89 lives at a rock concert in the Bataclan Theatre. The terrorist group ISIS/Daesh claimed responsibility for the massacre.

Postcolonialism: is an academic discipline that analyses the cultural legacy of colonialism. Many postcolonialist thinkers, such as Edward Said, argue that colonialist and Eurocentric views remain common in modern Western scholarship in general, and that these views undermine the intellectual validity of such scholarship.

Propaganda: deriving from the original Latin word meaning "to propagate," as in to spread or promote an idea, often benignly, propaganda today refers almost exclusively to the dissemination of one-sided, biased news or ideas, designed to manipulate the consumer's opinion in some way.

Renaissance: a movement that reinvigorated European culture at the end of the medieval period by turning toward the style and forms of the Classical world of pagan Greece and Rome.

Seljuk Turks: a people who migrated from central Asia into Persia in the tenth century, then gradually took control of Persia and areas of Anatolia, Mesopotamia, and the Levant. By the time of the Crusades, the Seljuks were a powerful, if divided, military and political force in and around the Holy Land.

Sicily: in the ninth century, Muslim forces conquered Sicily and established the Emirate of Sicily. Although the Normans recaptured Sicily in the eleventh century, Muslims remained an important part of the island's society and politics for another 200 years.

Sufism: a movement and school of thought within Islam that uses focus on an inner mysticism or spirit to remove all distractions but Allah, intensifying faith and so moving further to true *ihsan* (perfection of worship).

Umayyad Caliphate: an empire, headed by the Umayyad family, which ruled the Muslim world between 661 and 750. Their territory stretched from Iberia, across North Africa, and throughout the Middle East. In 750, the Umayyads were deposed from their capital in Damascus by the Abbasids. Caliphate refers to a state or government where the leader is titled "caliph," or successor, to the prophet of Islam, Muhammad. Though the forms of government and level of adherence to Islamic law have varied over the centuries in places where caliphates have been declared (for instance, with regard to alcohol), they are invariably ruled by some form of Sharia, or religious, law.

War on Terror: the name used by the American government to refer to the military campaigns in various locations around the world that were led by the United States following the September 11 terrorist attacks in 2001.

World War I: the global conflict of 1914–18 fought between the Central Powers (Germany, Austria-Hungary, and the Ottoman Empire) and the victorious Allied Powers (Britain, France, Russia, and, after 1917, the United States). More than 16 million people died as a result of the war.

World War II: the global conflict of 1939–45 fought between the Axis Powers (Germany, Italy, and Japan) and the victorious Allied Powers (United Kingdom and its colonies, France, the former Soviet Union, and the United States).

Zionism: a movement, most active in the late nineteenth and early twentieth centuries, that lobbied for the establishment of a Jewish homeland in Palestine.

PEOPLE MENTIONED IN THE TEXT

Tahir Abbas (b. 1970) is a professor of sociology, and an academic and government consultant, based at Fatih University in Istanbul, Turkey. His research focuses on the experiences of Muslim minorities in the modern world (especially Britain). He looks in particular at the topics of multiculturalism and extremism.

Ibn al-Adim (1192–1262) was an Arab biographer and historian from the city of Aleppo in Syria, whose work focused on the history of Aleppo.

Muhammad Shahid Alam (b. 1950) is an economist and social scientist. Born in East Pakistan (modern–day Bangladesh) and educated in Pakistan and Canada, he is currently professor of economics at Northeastern University in Boston, Massachusetts. His work focuses on how former colonies are affected by Western foreign and economic policies.

Aristotle (384–322 B.C.E.) was a Greek philosopher and scientist. He was the first person known to theorize on the origins of money, claiming that it arose spontaneously as a solution to the inconveniences of barter.

Fayid Hammad Muhammad 'Ashur is an Arab scholar, whose work focuses on the role jihad played in fighting against the Crusaders. He is best known for his text, *Islamic Jihad against the Crusaders and Mongols in the Mamluk Period* (1995).

Ali ibn al-Athir (1160–1233) was an Arabic historian from Turkey, a follower of Saladin who travelled widely, and the author of a key world history book, the *al-Kamil fi'l-Ta'rikh* (*The Complete History*).

Jose Maria Aznar (b. 1953) was the prime minister of Spain from 1996 to 2004.

Malcolm Barber (b. 1943) is a British scholar of medieval history and emeritus professor at the University of Reading, UK. He is best known for his books, *The Trial of the Templars* (1978) and *The New Knighthood: A History of the Order of the Temple* (1994).

Geoffrey Barraclough (1908–84) was a British historian and scholar who initially focused on medieval Germany and the Papacy. He subsequently became a major commentator on contemporary history and the use of history in the social sciences.

Jonathan Berkey (b. 1959) is a Western scholar of the Middle East and Islam. Currently professor of international studies and history at Davidson University in the United States, he has particular interests in medieval Islam and how this can inform our understanding of the current situation in the Middle East.

George W. Bush (b. 1946) was the 43rd president of the United States. A Republican, he served two terms, from 2001 to 2009.

Paul Chevedden is a scholar of the Crusades and medieval Islam, and history lecturer at UCLA, California. His research has included a discussion of relations between Muslims and Christians in the Holy Land and Spain. He has also worked on both Christian and Muslim perceptions of the Crusades.

Niall Christie is a lecturer at Langara College, Vancouver, Canada and the author of *Muslims and Crusaders: Christianity's Wars in the Middle East, 1095–1382, from the Islamic Sources* (2014). He reviewed *The Crusades: Islamic Perspectives* for the *Times Literary Supplement*.

Mahmud Darwish (1942–2008) was a Palestinian-born poet and writer, who is celebrated as one of the leading poets of the Palestinian diaspora.

Shira Fishman is an American psychologist at William James College, Massachusetts, whose work focuses on the psychology of terrorism.

Francesco Gabrieli (1904–96) was an Italian scholar specialising in the Middle East during the Crusading period. He was an expert in Arabic and much of his work focused on the translation and use of Arabic sources.

Muammar Gaddafi (1942–2011) was a Libyan military officer who seized power in Libya in 1969 and ruled as a dictator until he was overthrown and killed in 2011 during the Arab Spring.

Robert Hillenbrand is a scholar of Islamic art and architecture based at the University of Edinburgh, Scotland. He has undertaken studies in this field in Persia, the Levant, and North Africa. He has also worked on Islamic perceptions of other faiths.

Saddam Hussein (1937–2006) was a Ba'thist political figure, who seized the presidency of Iraq in 1979 and ruled as a dictator until 2003, when he was overthrown during the US-led invasion.

Jum'ah Muhammad Mustafá Jindi is a notable Islamic scholar and author of *Crusader Colonization in Palestine* (2006)

Ibn Jubayr (1145–1217) was a poet and writer from al Andalus, the name given to Islamic Spain, who traveled widely throughout the Mediterranean region, including the Crusader lands of the Levant, in the twelfth century. He wrote detailed accounts of his travels, which today are an invaluable record of life in the Islamic world at the height of the medieval period.

Arie Kruglanski (b. 1939) is a Polish-born psychologist at the University of Maryland, USA.

Osama bin Laden (1957–2011) was a Saudi Islamic radical responsible for the creation of al-Qaeda, the militant Islamic group that launched the 9/11 terrorist attacks.

Amin Maalouf (b. 1949) was born in Lebanon and now lives in France. After studying sociology and economics, he has written on the Crusades, and his knowledge of Arabic has allowed him access to an extensive range of materials that are underused in Western scholarship.

Muhammad al-'Arusi al-Matwi (1920–2005) was a Tunisian scholar and historian whose works included *al-Huroub al-salibah fi-al-mashriq wa-al-maghrib* (*The Crusading Wars, or The Wars of the Cross*), published in 1954.

Usama ibn Munqidh (1095–1188) was a Syrian historian, poet, and soldier, whose writings were contemporary to the Crusades.

David Nicolle (b. 1944) is a British military historian with an interest in the Crusades and warfare in the medieval Middle East. He has written a prodigious number of volumes dealing with military history and has collaborated with various pivotal authors.

Isabel O'Connor is a Spanish historian based at Cabrillo College, California, whose work focuses on the history of Muslims in medieval Spain.

Jonathan Phillips is professor of Crusading history at Royal Holloway University, London. His most recent work considers the relevance of the Crusades to the modern world.

J. M. B. Porter is a professor of global and historical studies at Butler University, Indiana.

Khurram Qadir is an important Pakistani scholar of the Crusades. He focuses in particular on the relevance of the Crusades to the modern world.

Donald Richards is a retired lecturer at the Oxford Oriental Institute, UK, where he taught Carole Hillenbrand during her studies. He continues to publish works on Islamic sources for the Crusades.

Jonathan Riley-Smith (b. 1938) is a fellow of Emmanuel College, Cambridge, and a prominent historian of the Crusades. During his extensive career he has focused on the military history of the Crusades, and researched fields as diverse as the politics and society of the Crusader states, and theology and canon law.

Susan Rose is a former senior research fellow at Roehampton University, UK, whose work focused on medieval naval warfare.

Steven Runciman (1903–2000) was a British historian specializing in the Crusades. His seminal book *A History of the Crusades*, 3 vols. (1951–4) was highly influential and remains a valuable resource for students of the Crusades. However some recent critics claim his work is outdated and Eurocentric.

Edward Said (1935–2003) was a Palestinian American literary critic best known for his critical analysis of Western academia's presentations of the rest of the world. A noted political activist and supporter of the two-state solution for the Israel–Palestine conflict, he was also a key figure in the foundation of postcolonialist theory.

Saladin (circa 1137–93) was an Islamic leader of Kurdish background who successfully united Egypt and Syria into one state under his rule, decisively defeated the Crusader states and reclaimed Jerusalem for the Islamic faith. Though he failed to defeat Richard of England in battle during the Third Crusade, he successfully held Jerusalem. As a result Richard's Crusade was deemed a failure.

Abu Shama (1203–67) was a Syrian historian who transcribed many of the official documents produced during Saladin's reign and wrote on the Arab perspective of the Crusades.

Emmanuel Sivan is a historian of the Middle East specialising in Islamic fundamentalism and Middle Eastern politics, and is professor of Islamic history at the Hebrew University of Jerusalem, Israel. He appears regularly in Israeli media providing commentary on Islamic movements.

Ali ibn Tahir al-Sulami (d. 1106) was a Syrian scholar who was the first to preach jihad against the crusaders, in his 1105 treatise *Book of Jihad*.

Yasir Suleiman is a Palestinian Arab scholar of the modern Middle East, currently professor of modern Arabic studies at the University of Cambridge. He has written extensively on the Arabic language and politics, and is internationally acclaimed for his work.

Giles Tremlett (b. 1962) is a British author and journalist, best known for his book *Ghosts of Spain: Travels Through a Country's Hidden Past* (2007).

Christopher Tyerman is a British professor of history at Hertford College, Oxford, and author of *God's War: A New History of the Crusades* (2006).

Pope Urban II (circa 1042–99) was born in France and led the Roman Catholic Church from 1088 until 1099. He initiated the First Crusade after an appeal for assistance from the Byzantine Emperor Alexius I Comnenus, an Orthodox Christian who was under attack from Muslim Seljuk Turkish invaders. Urban called an Ecumenical Council and urged all Catholics to reclaim Jerusalem from the Muslims, offering those who succeeded absolution from sins.

Mark Woodward is an American academic who has studied Islamic history for over 30 years. He is a professor of history at Arizona State University and has written *Islam in Java: Normative Piety and Mysticism in the Sultanate of Yogyakarta* (1989) and *Java, Indonesia, and Islam* (2010).

Suhayl Zakkar is a scholar of the Crusades, best known for his book *The Emirate of Aleppo, 1004–1094* (1971).

Imad ad-Din Zengi (circa 1085–1146) was a Turkish leader who ruled much of what is now Syria and Iraq. He repeatedly fought the Crusaders, and later Muslim scholars argued that Zengi's recapture of the Crusader state "County of Edessa" started both the Second Crusade and a wider jihad against all the Crusader states.

WORKS CITED

WORKS CITED

Abbas, Tahir. "Islamophobia and the Politics of Young British Muslim Ethno-Religious Identities." In *Youth Work and Islam: A Leap of Faith for Young People*, edited by Brian Belton and Sadek Hamid, 53–71. Rotterdam: Sense Publishers, 2011.

Alam, M. Shahid, R. Bin Wong, Jack A. Goldstone, and Ricardo Duchesne. "Eurocentrism, Sinocentrism and World History: A Symposium." *Science & Society* 67, no. 2 (Summer 2003): 173–217.

'Ashur, F. H. M. *Al-jihad al-islami didd al-salibiyyan wa'l-murghul fi'l-'asr almamluk* (Islamic jihad against the Crusaders and Mongols in the Mamluk period). Tripoli, Lebanon: Jros Press, 1995.

Barber, Malcolm. "Review of *The Crusades: Islamic Perspectives*." *History Today* (2000). Accessed December 10, 2015. http://www.historytoday.com/malcolm-barber/crusades-islamic-perspectives.

Barraclough, Geoffrey. "Deus le Volt?" *The New York Review of Books*, May 21, 1970. Accessed December 10, 2015. http://www.nybooks.com/articles/1970/05/21/deus-le-volt/.

Berkey, Jonathan P. "Review of *The Crusades: Islamic Perspectives*." *International Journal of Middle East Studies* 34, no. 1 (2002): 129–31.

Brewer, Harry. "Historical Perspectives on Health: Early Arabic Medicine." *The Journal of the Royal Society for the Promotion of Health* 124, no. 4 (2004): 184–7.

Chevedden, Paul E. "The Islamic View and the Christian View of the Crusades: A New Synthesis." *History* 93, no. 310 (April 2008): 181–200.

Christie, Niall. *Muslims and Crusaders: Christianity's Wars in the Middle East,*

1095–1382, from the Islamic Sources. Abingdon: Routledge, 2014.

Cobb, Paul M. *The Race for Paradise: An Islamic History of the Crusades.* Oxford: Oxford University Press, 2014.

Ford, Peter. "Europe cringes at Bush 'crusade' against terrorists." *Christian Science Monitor*, September 19, 2001. Accessed December 10, 2015. http://www.csmonitor.com/2001/0919/p12s2-woeu.html.

Gabrieli, Francesco. *Arab Historians of the Crusades*. Translated by E. J. Costello. New York: Routledge & Kegan Paul, 1969.

Hayes, Dawn Marie. "Harnessing the Potential in Historiography and Popular Culture When Teaching the Crusades." *The History Teacher* 40, no. 3 (May 2007): 349–61.

Hillenbrand, Carole. "The Arabic Sources." In *The Prosopography of the Byzantine Empire, 1024–1204,* edited by M. Whitby, 283–340. London: The British Academy, 2007.

————. "Aspects of Jihad Propaganda: The Evidence of Twelfth-Century Inscriptions." In *Proceedings of the Conference on the History of the Crusades*, 53–63. Bir Zeit: University of Bir Zeit, 1993.

————. *The Crusades: Islamic Perspectives.* Edinburgh: Edinburgh University Press, 1999.

————. "The Establishment of Artuqid power in Diyar Bakr in the Twelfth Century." *Studia Islamica* 54 (1981).

————. "The First Crusade: The Muslim Perspective." In *The Origins and Impact of the First Crusade*, edited by J. Phillips, 130–41. Manchester: Manchester University Press, 1997.

————. "The Islamic World and the Crusades." *Scottish Journal of Religious Studies* 8 (1987): 150–57.

————. *A Muslim Principality in Crusader Times: The Early Artuqid State.* Leiden: The Netherlands Historical and Archaeological Institute of the Near East in Istanbul, 1990.

————. "Some Medieval Islamic Approaches to Source Material." *Oriens* 27/8 (1981): 197–225.

————. "Some Medieval Muslim Views on Constantinople." In *World Christianity in Muslim Encounter: Essays in Memory of David A. Kerr* Vol.2. Edited by Stephen R. Goodwin. London: Continuum, 2009.

————. *Turkish Myth and Muslim Symbol: The Battle of Manzikert.* Edinburgh: Edinburgh University Press, 2007.

————. *The Waning of the Umayyad Caliphate.* Albany: State University of New York Press, 1989.

Jindi, Jum"ah Muhammad Mustafá. *Al-istitan al-salibi fi Filastin: 492–690 H./ 1099–1291 M.* (Crusader colonization in Palestine: 492–690AH / 1099– 1291CE). Cairo: Maktabat al-Anjulu al-Misriyah, 2006.

Kruglanski, Arie W., and Shira Fishman. "The Psychology of Terrorism: 'Syndrome' Versus 'Tool' Perspectives." *Terrorism and Political Violence* 18, no. 2 (2006): 193–215.

Maalouf, Amin. *The Crusades through Arab Eyes.* London: Al Saqi Books, 1984.

Nicolle, David. *The Crusades*. Oxford: Osprey, 2001.

O'Connor, Isabel A. "Review of *The Crusades: Islamic Perspectives*." *Islamic Studies* 42, no. 2 (Summer 2003): 357–60.

Phillips, Jonathan. *The Crusades 1095–1197*. Harlow: Pearson Education, 2002.

Porter, J. M. B. "Osama Bin-Laden, *Jihad*, and the Sources of International Terrorism." *Symposium: From Pipe Bombs to PhDs: International Terrorism in the Twenty-First Century. Indiana International and Comparative Law Review* 13 (2002–3): 871–85.

Qadir, Khurram. "Modern Historiography: The Relevance of the Crusades." *Islamic Studies* 46, no. 4 (Winter 2007): 527–58.

Queen Mary University of London. "Resources for Studying the Crusades." Accessed May 30, 2013. http://www.crusaderstudies.org.uk/resources/historians/profiles/hillenbrand/.

Riley-Smith, Jonathan. *The Crusades, Christianity and Islam*. New York: Columbia University Press, 2008.

— — —. *The Crusades: A Short History.* New Haven, CT: Yale University Press, 1987.

— — —. "History, the Crusades and the Latin East, 1095–1204: A Personal View." In *Crusaders and Muslims in Twelfth-Century Syria*, edited by M. Shatzmiller, 1–17. Leiden: Brill, 1993.

Rose, Susan. *Medieval Naval Warfare, 1000–1500.* London: Routledge, 2002.

Runciman, Steven. *A History of the Crusades*. 3 vols. Cambridge: Cambridge University Press, 1951–4.

Said, Edward. *Orientalism.* London: Vintage, 1978.

Simon, Evan. "Historians Weigh in on Obama's Comparison of ISIS Militants to Medieval Christian Crusaders." ABC News, February 6, 2015. Accessed December 8, 2015. http://abcnews.go.com/Politics/historians-weigh-obamas-comparison-isis-militants-medieval-christian/story?id=28787194.

Sivan, Emmanuel. "Modern Arab Historiography of the Crusades." *Asian and African Studies* 8, no. 2 (1972).

Suleiman, Yasir, ed. *Living Islamic History: Studies in Honour of Professor Carole Hillenbrand.* Edinburgh: Edinburgh University Press, 2010.

Thames and Hudson online catalogue information. "Introduction to Islamic Beliefs and Practices in Historical Perspective." Accessed October 21, 2015. http://www.thamesandhudsonusa.com/books/introduction-to-islam-beliefs-and-practices-in-historical-perspective-softcover

Tremlett, Giles. *Ghosts of Spain*. London: Faber and Faber, 2006.

Tyerman, Christopher. *God's War: A New History of the Crusades*. London: Penguin, 2007.

University of Edinburgh. "Professor Carole Hillenbrand." Accessed May 30, 2013. http://www.ed.ac.uk/literatures-languages-cultures/islamic-middle-eastern/people/c-hillenbrand.

University of Edinburgh. "Professor Robert Hillenbrand." Accessed May 31, 2013. http://www.ed.ac.uk/literatures-languages-cultures/islamic-middle-eastern/people/r-hillenbrand.

Woodward, Mark. "Tropes of the Crusades in Indonesian Muslim Discourse." *Contemporary Islam* 4, no. 3 (October 2010): 311–30.

Zakkar, Suhayl. *Madkhal ila ta'rikh al-hurub al-salibiyah* (Introduction to the history of the Crusades). Beirut: Dar al-Fikr, 1973.

THE MACAT LIBRARY
BY DISCIPLINE

The Macat Library By Discipline

AFRICANA STUDIES

Chinua Achebe's *An Image of Africa: Racism in Conrad's Heart of Darkness*
W. E. B. Du Bois's *The Souls of Black Folk*
Zora Neale Huston's *Characteristics of Negro Expression*
Martin Luther King Jr's *Why We Can't Wait*
Toni Morrison's *Playing in the Dark: Whiteness in the American Literary Imagination*

ANTHROPOLOGY

Arjun Appadurai's *Modernity at Large: Cultural Dimensions of Globalisation*
Philippe Ariès's *Centuries of Childhood*
Franz Boas's *Race, Language and Culture*
Kim Chan & Renée Mauborgne's *Blue Ocean Strategy*
Jared Diamond's *Guns, Germs & Steel: the Fate of Human Societies*
Jared Diamond's *Collapse: How Societies Choose to Fail or Survive*
E. E. Evans-Pritchard's *Witchcraft, Oracles and Magic Among the Azande*
James Ferguson's *The Anti-Politics Machine*
Clifford Geertz's *The Interpretation of Cultures*
David Graeber's *Debt: the First 5000 Years*
Karen Ho's *Liquidated: An Ethnography of Wall Street*
Geert Hofstede's *Culture's Consequences: Comparing Values, Behaviors, Institutes and Organizations across Nations*
Claude Lévi-Strauss's *Structural Anthropology*
Jay Macleod's *Ain't No Makin' It: Aspirations and Attainment in a Low-Income Neighborhood*
Saba Mahmood's *The Politics of Piety: The Islamic Revival and the Feminist Subject*
Marcel Mauss's *The Gift*

BUSINESS

Jean Lave & Etienne Wenger's *Situated Learning*
Theodore Levitt's *Marketing Myopia*
Burton G. Malkiel's *A Random Walk Down Wall Street*
Douglas McGregor's *The Human Side of Enterprise*
Michael Porter's *Competitive Strategy: Creating and Sustaining Superior Performance*
John Kotter's *Leading Change*
C. K. Prahalad & Gary Hamel's *The Core Competence of the Corporation*

CRIMINOLOGY

Michelle Alexander's *The New Jim Crow: Mass Incarceration in the Age of Colorblindness*
Michael R. Gottfredson & Travis Hirschi's *A General Theory of Crime*
Richard Herrnstein & Charles A. Murray's *The Bell Curve: Intelligence and Class Structure in American Life*
Elizabeth Loftus's *Eyewitness Testimony*
Jay Macleod's *Ain't No Makin' It: Aspirations and Attainment in a Low-Income Neighborhood*
Philip Zimbardo's *The Lucifer Effect*

ECONOMICS

Janet Abu-Lughod's *Before European Hegemony*
Ha-Joon Chang's *Kicking Away the Ladder*
David Brion Davis's *The Problem of Slavery in the Age of Revolution*
Milton Friedman's *The Role of Monetary Policy*
Milton Friedman's *Capitalism and Freedom*
David Graeber's *Debt: the First 5000 Years*
Friedrich Hayek's *The Road to Serfdom*
Karen Ho's *Liquidated: An Ethnography of Wall Street*

John Maynard Keynes's *The General Theory of Employment, Interest and Money*
Charles P. Kindleberger's *Manias, Panics and Crashes*
Robert Lucas's *Why Doesn't Capital Flow from Rich to Poor Countries?*
Burton G. Malkiel's *A Random Walk Down Wall Street*
Thomas Robert Malthus's *An Essay on the Principle of Population*
Karl Marx's *Capital*
Thomas Piketty's *Capital in the Twenty-First Century*
Amartya Sen's *Development as Freedom*
Adam Smith's *The Wealth of Nations*
Nassim Nicholas Taleb's *The Black Swan: The Impact of the Highly Improbable*
Amos Tversky's & Daniel Kahneman's *Judgment under Uncertainty: Heuristics and Biases*
Mahbub Ul Haq's *Reflections on Human Development*
Max Weber's *The Protestant Ethic and the Spirit of Capitalism*

FEMINISM AND GENDER STUDIES

Judith Butler's *Gender Trouble*
Simone De Beauvoir's *The Second Sex*
Michel Foucault's *History of Sexuality*
Betty Friedan's *The Feminine Mystique*
Saba Mahmood's *The Politics of Piety: The Islamic Revival and the Feminist Subject*
Joan Wallach Scott's *Gender and the Politics of History*
Mary Wollstonecraft's *A Vindication of the Rights of Woman*
Virginia Woolf's *A Room of One's Own*

GEOGRAPHY

The Brundtland Report's *Our Common Future*
Rachel Carson's *Silent Spring*
Charles Darwin's *On the Origin of Species*
James Ferguson's *The Anti-Politics Machine*
Jane Jacobs's *The Death and Life of Great American Cities*
James Lovelock's *Gaia: A New Look at Life on Earth*
Amartya Sen's *Development as Freedom*
Mathis Wackernagel & William Rees's *Our Ecological Footprint*

HISTORY

Janet Abu-Lughod's *Before European Hegemony*
Benedict Anderson's *Imagined Communities*
Bernard Bailyn's *The Ideological Origins of the American Revolution*
Hanna Batatu's *The Old Social Classes And The Revolutionary Movements Of Iraq*
Christopher Browning's *Ordinary Men: Reserve Police Batallion 101 and the Final Solution in Poland*
Edmund Burke's *Reflections on the Revolution in France*
William Cronon's *Nature's Metropolis: Chicago And The Great West*
Alfred W. Crosby's *The Columbian Exchange*
Hamid Dabashi's *Iran: A People Interrupted*
David Brion Davis's *The Problem of Slavery in the Age of Revolution*
Nathalie Zemon Davis's *The Return of Martin Guerre*
Jared Diamond's *Guns, Germs & Steel: the Fate of Human Societies*
Frank Dikotter's *Mao's Great Famine*
John W Dower's *War Without Mercy: Race And Power In The Pacific War*
W. E. B. Du Bois's *The Souls of Black Folk*
Richard J. Evans's *In Defence of History*
Lucien Febvre's *The Problem of Unbelief in the 16th Century*
Sheila Fitzpatrick's *Everyday Stalinism*

Eric Foner's *Reconstruction: America's Unfinished Revolution, 1863-1877*
Michel Foucault's *Discipline and Punish*
Michel Foucault's *History of Sexuality*
Francis Fukuyama's *The End of History and the Last Man*
John Lewis Gaddis's *We Now Know: Rethinking Cold War History*
Ernest Gellner's *Nations and Nationalism*
Eugene Genovese's *Roll, Jordan, Roll: The World the Slaves Made*
Carlo Ginzburg's *The Night Battles*
Daniel Goldhagen's *Hitler's Willing Executioners*
Jack Goldstone's *Revolution and Rebellion in the Early Modern World*
Antonio Gramsci's *The Prison Notebooks*
Alexander Hamilton, John Jay & James Madison's *The Federalist Papers*
Christopher Hill's *The World Turned Upside Down*
Carole Hillenbrand's *The Crusades: Islamic Perspectives*
Thomas Hobbes's *Leviathan*
Eric Hobsbawm's *The Age Of Revolution*
John A. Hobson's *Imperialism: A Study*
Albert Hourani's *History of the Arab Peoples*
Samuel P. Huntington's *The Clash of Civilizations and the Remaking of World Order*
C. L. R. James's *The Black Jacobins*
Tony Judt's *Postwar: A History of Europe Since 1945*
Ernst Kantorowicz's *The King's Two Bodies: A Study in Medieval Political Theology*
Paul Kennedy's *The Rise and Fall of the Great Powers*
Ian Kershaw's *The "Hitler Myth": Image and Reality in the Third Reich*
John Maynard Keynes's *The General Theory of Employment, Interest and Money*
Charles P. Kindleberger's *Manias, Panics and Crashes*
Martin Luther King Jr's *Why We Can't Wait*
Henry Kissinger's *World Order: Reflections on the Character of Nations and the Course of History*
Thomas Kuhn's *The Structure of Scientific Revolutions*
Georges Lefebvre's *The Coming of the French Revolution*
John Locke's *Two Treatises of Government*
Niccolò Machiavelli's *The Prince*
Thomas Robert Malthus's *An Essay on the Principle of Population*
Mahmood Mamdani's *Citizen and Subject: Contemporary Africa And The Legacy Of Late Colonialism*
Karl Marx's *Capital*
Stanley Milgram's *Obedience to Authority*
John Stuart Mill's *On Liberty*
Thomas Paine's *Common Sense*
Thomas Paine's *Rights of Man*
Geoffrey Parker's *Global Crisis: War, Climate Change and Catastrophe in the Seventeenth Century*
Jonathan Riley-Smith's *The First Crusade and the Idea of Crusading*
Jean-Jacques Rousseau's *The Social Contract*
Joan Wallach Scott's *Gender and the Politics of History*
Theda Skocpol's *States and Social Revolutions*
Adam Smith's *The Wealth of Nations*
Timothy Snyder's *Bloodlands: Europe Between Hitler and Stalin*
Sun Tzu's *The Art of War*
Keith Thomas's *Religion and the Decline of Magic*
Thucydides's *The History of the Peloponnesian War*
Frederick Jackson Turner's *The Significance of the Frontier in American History*
Odd Arne Westad's *The Global Cold War: Third World Interventions And The Making Of Our Times*

LITERATURE

Chinua Achebe's *An Image of Africa: Racism in Conrad's Heart of Darkness*
Roland Barthes's *Mythologies*
Homi K. Bhabha's *The Location of Culture*
Judith Butler's *Gender Trouble*
Simone De Beauvoir's *The Second Sex*
Ferdinand De Saussure's *Course in General Linguistics*
T. S. Eliot's *The Sacred Wood: Essays on Poetry and Criticism*
Zora Neale Huston's *Characteristics of Negro Expression*
Toni Morrison's *Playing in the Dark: Whiteness in the American Literary Imagination*
Edward Said's *Orientalism*
Gayatri Chakravorty Spivak's *Can the Subaltern Speak?*
Mary Wollstonecraft's *A Vindication of the Rights of Women*
Virginia Woolf's *A Room of One's Own*

PHILOSOPHY

Elizabeth Anscombe's *Modern Moral Philosophy*
Hannah Arendt's *The Human Condition*
Aristotle's *Metaphysics*
Aristotle's *Nicomachean Ethics*
Edmund Gettier's *Is Justified True Belief Knowledge?*
Georg Wilhelm Friedrich Hegel's *Phenomenology of Spirit*
David Hume's *Dialogues Concerning Natural Religion*
David Hume's *The Enquiry for Human Understanding*
Immanuel Kant's *Religion within the Boundaries of Mere Reason*
Immanuel Kant's *Critique of Pure Reason*
Søren Kierkegaard's *The Sickness Unto Death*
Søren Kierkegaard's *Fear and Trembling*
C. S. Lewis's *The Abolition of Man*
Alasdair MacIntyre's *After Virtue*
Marcus Aurelius's *Meditations*
Friedrich Nietzsche's *On the Genealogy of Morality*
Friedrich Nietzsche's *Beyond Good and Evil*
Plato's *Republic*
Plato's *Symposium*
Jean-Jacques Rousseau's *The Social Contract*
Gilbert Ryle's *The Concept of Mind*
Baruch Spinoza's *Ethics*
Sun Tzu's *The Art of War*
Ludwig Wittgenstein's *Philosophical Investigations*

POLITICS

Benedict Anderson's *Imagined Communities*
Aristotle's *Politics*
Bernard Bailyn's *The Ideological Origins of the American Revolution*
Edmund Burke's *Reflections on the Revolution in France*
John C. Calhoun's *A Disquisition on Government*
Ha-Joon Chang's *Kicking Away the Ladder*
Hamid Dabashi's *Iran: A People Interrupted*
Hamid Dabashi's *Theology of Discontent: The Ideological Foundation of the Islamic Revolution in Iran*
Robert Dahl's *Democracy and its Critics*
Robert Dahl's *Who Governs?*
David Brion Davis's *The Problem of Slavery in the Age of Revolution*

The Macat Library By Discipline

Alexis De Tocqueville's *Democracy in America*
James Ferguson's *The Anti-Politics Machine*
Frank Dikotter's *Mao's Great Famine*
Sheila Fitzpatrick's *Everyday Stalinism*
Eric Foner's *Reconstruction: America's Unfinished Revolution, 1863-1877*
Milton Friedman's *Capitalism and Freedom*
Francis Fukuyama's *The End of History and the Last Man*
John Lewis Gaddis's *We Now Know: Rethinking Cold War History*
Ernest Gellner's *Nations and Nationalism*
David Graeber's *Debt: the First 5000 Years*
Antonio Gramsci's *The Prison Notebooks*
Alexander Hamilton, John Jay & James Madison's *The Federalist Papers*
Friedrich Hayek's *The Road to Serfdom*
Christopher Hill's *The World Turned Upside Down*
Thomas Hobbes's *Leviathan*
John A. Hobson's *Imperialism: A Study*
Samuel P. Huntington's *The Clash of Civilizations and the Remaking of World Order*
Tony Judt's *Postwar: A History of Europe Since 1945*
David C. Kang's *China Rising: Peace, Power and Order in East Asia*
Paul Kennedy's *The Rise and Fall of Great Powers*
Robert Keohane's *After Hegemony*
Martin Luther King Jr.'s *Why We Can't Wait*
Henry Kissinger's *World Order: Reflections on the Character of Nations and the Course of History*
John Locke's *Two Treatises of Government*
Niccolò Machiavelli's *The Prince*
Thomas Robert Malthus's *An Essay on the Principle of Population*
Mahmood Mamdani's *Citizen and Subject: Contemporary Africa And The Legacy Of Late Colonialism*
Karl Marx's *Capital*
John Stuart Mill's *On Liberty*
John Stuart Mill's *Utilitarianism*
Hans Morgenthau's *Politics Among Nations*
Thomas Paine's *Common Sense*
Thomas Paine's *Rights of Man*
Thomas Piketty's *Capital in the Twenty-First Century*
Robert D. Putman's *Bowling Alone*
John Rawls's *Theory of Justice*
Jean-Jacques Rousseau's *The Social Contract*
Theda Skocpol's *States and Social Revolutions*
Adam Smith's *The Wealth of Nations*
Sun Tzu's *The Art of War*
Henry David Thoreau's *Civil Disobedience*
Thucydides's *The History of the Peloponnesian War*
Kenneth Waltz's *Theory of International Politics*
Max Weber's *Politics as a Vocation*
Odd Arne Westad's *The Global Cold War: Third World Interventions And The Making Of Our Times*

POSTCOLONIAL STUDIES

Roland Barthes's *Mythologies*
Frantz Fanon's *Black Skin, White Masks*
Homi K. Bhabha's *The Location of Culture*
Gustavo Gutiérrez's *A Theology of Liberation*
Edward Said's *Orientalism*
Gayatri Chakravorty Spivak's *Can the Subaltern Speak?*

PSYCHOLOGY

Gordon Allport's *The Nature of Prejudice*
Alan Baddeley & Graham Hitch's *Aggression: A Social Learning Analysis*
Albert Bandura's *Aggression: A Social Learning Analysis*
Leon Festinger's *A Theory of Cognitive Dissonance*
Sigmund Freud's *The Interpretation of Dreams*
Betty Friedan's *The Feminine Mystique*
Michael R. Gottfredson & Travis Hirschi's *A General Theory of Crime*
Eric Hoffer's *The True Believer: Thoughts on the Nature of Mass Movements*
William James's *Principles of Psychology*
Elizabeth Loftus's *Eyewitness Testimony*
A. H. Maslow's *A Theory of Human Motivation*
Stanley Milgram's *Obedience to Authority*
Steven Pinker's *The Better Angels of Our Nature*
Oliver Sacks's *The Man Who Mistook His Wife For a Hat*
Richard Thaler & Cass Sunstein's *Nudge: Improving Decisions About Health, Wealth and Happiness*
Amos Tversky's *Judgment under Uncertainty: Heuristics and Biases*
Philip Zimbardo's *The Lucifer Effect*

SCIENCE

Rachel Carson's *Silent Spring*
William Cronon's *Nature's Metropolis: Chicago And The Great West*
Alfred W. Crosby's *The Columbian Exchange*
Charles Darwin's *On the Origin of Species*
Richard Dawkin's *The Selfish Gene*
Thomas Kuhn's *The Structure of Scientific Revolutions*
Geoffrey Parker's *Global Crisis: War, Climate Change and Catastrophe in the Seventeenth Century*
Mathis Wackernagel & William Rees's *Our Ecological Footprint*

SOCIOLOGY

Michelle Alexander's *The New Jim Crow: Mass Incarceration in the Age of Colorblindness*
Gordon Allport's *The Nature of Prejudice*
Albert Bandura's *Aggression: A Social Learning Analysis*
Hanna Batatu's *The Old Social Classes And The Revolutionary Movements Of Iraq*
Ha-Joon Chang's *Kicking Away the Ladder*
W. E. B. Du Bois's *The Souls of Black Folk*
Émile Durkheim's *On Suicide*
Frantz Fanon's *Black Skin, White Masks*
Frantz Fanon's *The Wretched of the Earth*
Eric Foner's *Reconstruction: America's Unfinished Revolution, 1863-1877*
Eugene Genovese's *Roll, Jordan, Roll: The World the Slaves Made*
Jack Goldstone's *Revolution and Rebellion in the Early Modern World*
Antonio Gramsci's *The Prison Notebooks*
Richard Herrnstein & Charles A Murray's *The Bell Curve: Intelligence and Class Structure in American Life*
Eric Hoffer's *The True Believer: Thoughts on the Nature of Mass Movements*
Jane Jacobs's *The Death and Life of Great American Cities*
Robert Lucas's *Why Doesn't Capital Flow from Rich to Poor Countries?*
Jay Macleod's *Ain't No Makin' It: Aspirations and Attainment in a Low Income Neighborhood*
Elaine May's *Homeward Bound: American Families in the Cold War Era*
Douglas McGregor's *The Human Side of Enterprise*
C. Wright Mills's *The Sociological Imagination*

The Macat Library By Discipline

Thomas Piketty's *Capital in the Twenty-First Century*
Robert D. Putman's *Bowling Alone*
David Riesman's *The Lonely Crowd: A Study of the Changing American Character*
Edward Said's *Orientalism*
Joan Wallach Scott's *Gender and the Politics of History*
Theda Skocpol's *States and Social Revolutions*
Max Weber's *The Protestant Ethic and the Spirit of Capitalism*

THEOLOGY

Augustine's *Confessions*
Benedict's *Rule of St Benedict*
Gustavo Gutiérrez's *A Theology of Liberation*
Carole Hillenbrand's *The Crusades: Islamic Perspectives*
David Hume's *Dialogues Concerning Natural Religion*
Immanuel Kant's *Religion within the Boundaries of Mere Reason*
Ernst Kantorowicz's *The King's Two Bodies: A Study in Medieval Political Theology*
Søren Kierkegaard's *The Sickness Unto Death*
C. S. Lewis's *The Abolition of Man*
Saba Mahmood's *The Politics of Piety: The Islamic Revival and the Feminist Subject*
Baruch Spinoza's *Ethics*
Keith Thomas's *Religion and the Decline of Magic*

COMING SOON

Chris Argyris's *The Individual and the Organisation*
Seyla Benhabib's *The Rights of Others*
Walter Benjamin's *The Work Of Art in the Age of Mechanical Reproduction*
John Berger's *Ways of Seeing*
Pierre Bourdieu's *Outline of a Theory of Practice*
Mary Douglas's *Purity and Danger*
Roland Dworkin's *Taking Rights Seriously*
James G. March's *Exploration and Exploitation in Organisational Learning*
Ikujiro Nonaka's *A Dynamic Theory of Organizational Knowledge Creation*
Griselda Pollock's *Vision and Difference*
Amartya Sen's *Inequality Re-Examined*
Susan Sontag's *On Photography*
Yasser Tabbaa's *The Transformation of Islamic Art*
Ludwig von Mises's *Theory of Money and Credit*

Printed in the United States
by Baker & Taylor Publisher Services